IDENTITY CRISIS!

JEFF FISHER

IDENTITY CRISIS!

50 redesigns that transformed
stale identities into successful brands

letterhead, logos, websites and more

HOW
BOOKS
Cincinnati, Ohio
www.howdesign.com

EDITED BY:
Amy Schell

DESIGNED BY:
Grace Ring

PRODUCTION COORDINATED BY:
Greg Nock

For more fine books from F+W Publications, visit www.fwbookstore.com.

11 10 09 08 07   5 4 3 2 1

Distributed in Canada by Fraser Direct, 100 Armstrong Avenue, Georgetown, Ontario, Canada L7G 5S4, Tel: (905) 877-4411.

Distributed in the U.K. and Europe by David & Charles, Brunel House, Newton Abbot, Devon, TQ12 4PU, England, Tel: (+44) 1626-323200, Fax: (+44) 1626-323319, E-mail: postmaster@davidandcharles.co.uk.

Distributed in Australia by Capricorn Link, P.O. Box 704, Windsor, NSW 2756 Australia, Tel: (02) 4577-3555.

Library of Congress Cataloging-in-Publication Data

Fisher, Jeff, 1956-
  Identity crisis! : 50 redesigns that transformed stale identities into successful brands / by Jeff Fisher.
     p. cm.
  ISBN-13: 978-1-58180-939-8 (hardcover : alk. paper)
  1. Trademarks--Design. 2. Logos (Symbols)--Design. 3. Corporate image--Design. I. Title.
  NC1003.F57 2007
   741.6--dc22   2007008524

ABOUT THE AUTHOR

∧ Photo courtesy of Vicki Grayland

Jeff Fisher, Engineer of Creative Identity for the one-person design shop Jeff Fisher LogoMotives, has been designing logos, creating corporate identity systems and branding organizations, businesses and products for over thirty years. His clients have included one-person companies, small businesses, restaurants, hotels, education facilities, nonprofit organizations, government agencies, professional sports teams and major international corporations.

Fisher has received over 575 regional, national and international design awards for his logo and corporate identity efforts. His work has been featured in nearly 100 books and publications about logos, the business of graphic design and small business marketing.

Fisher serves on the *HOW* magazine editorial advisory board, the UCDA designer magazine editorial advisory board, the HOW design conference advisory council, and the management team of CreativeLatitude.com. A prolific writer, his articles and essays have appeared in *HOW* magazine, other design and business publications, numerous online design industry resources and on his blog, www.blog-omotives.blogspot.com.

The author of *The Savvy Designer's Guide to Success: Ideas and tactics for a killer career* (HOW Books, 2004), Fisher often can be found preaching what he practices through speaking engagements at creative industry conferences, colleges and business events around the country.

Jeff Fisher lives in Portland, Oregon, with his partner Ed Cunningham—and works from wherever he and his Apple PowerBook may be at any given time.

DEDICATION

I dedicate this book to my husband and best friend, Ed Cunningham, who has helped me identify what is most important in life over the past seventeen years—and is always there to lend a hand, an ear, or a kick in the rear during a crisis.

This volume is also written in memory of four friends who lost their hard-fought battles with various medical conditions in 2005. David Coyle, Brad Hall, Sharon Nixon and Glo Raineri were always very interested in and supportive of my design-related efforts and provided a great deal of professional and personal inspiration over the years. I also wish to honor the creative spirit of my friend, web developer and photographer, Walt Nixon.

TABLE OF CONTENTS

IDENTITY REDESIGNS

"THE LOGO IS THE POINT
OF ENTRY FOR THE BRAND."

—Milton Glaser

Foreword

In a world of constantly evolving trends and attitudes, it can be hard for businesses to stay current in a market where consumers are always looking for the next best thing.

Identity design is an acknowledged business weapon for companies—a strategic asset, the written and visual expression of a company's product or service. But what happens when the way a company does business changes, but their identity doesn't evolve with them? Or worse, they update their identity, but their internal business structure remains the same? Either way, those companies take the risk of losing their customers' confidence for not delivering what they are promising.

In the past, an identity's shelf life was 20-30 years. The globe was bigger and change was slower. There was patience and tolerance for that. The value system skewed more toward stability, heritage and grounded companies. By 1999 we'd reached the antithesis of that.

People's desires were for company images to reflect what's new, contemporary and relevant; to be agile with the culture, and to have an attitude that says, "We've got to be fresh and plugged in, now!" Today we live in a culture that expects and wants change. We want choices and are impatient for anything new and improved.

So, is the role of identity to signal stability or relevance? If the business is stable and relevant, there probably isn't a need to re-brand. If it's stable, but not relevant, it should be evolved to be more in tune with the present. The identity needs to have a grounded foundation, but also the speed, agility and relevance of today.

With rare exceptions, it's important to evolve every identity over time. However, the degree of change should be commensurate with how much you want someone to recognize that change. Examples of this are found with Morton Salt, Coke, Pepsi and IBM, which have all evolved their look many times over the years in incremental updates, maintaining a confidence in consumers' minds. They evolved each brand to be fresher and more relevant, but in modest steps, focusing on subtle, intuitive shifts.

In some instances, however, specific businesses are expected to change. This is especially seen in categories of business and industry that are more ephemeral, such as fashion and some technology. These industries must demonstrate timely relevance, so their brand evolution needs to be more noticeable, serving as a clue for consumers to recognize this is something new. The very brand purpose is to present itself as being current, so the refresh of the brand is more obvious.

But, it doesn't do any good to re-brand unless it's an accurate reflection of how a company is changing. If a company just changes its graphics and nothing operationally, it hurts itself by developing expectations on which it can't deliver. The evolution should start from the inside then be expressed externally. Regardless of reason for re-brand, change without re-educating one's customers on the new brand can only cultivate distrust and confusion.

While it's important to ask the big question of whether or not to re-brand, it takes discipline to answer the question in a responsible way and produce an equally responsible evolution. If the change is too small, you're not getting the value out of it and no one notices. You need to push the evolution slightly out of your comfort zone, yet still make it appropriate to allow your company room to grow into it, while maximizing its shelf life.

Ultimately, the critical paradigm is to address your re-brand with the relevance of today, without sacrificing the core equities your business represents.

Jack Anderson
Founding Partner
& Creative Director
Hornall Anderson Design

Introduction

A graphic identity crisis does not happen only to multinational corporations whose rebranding efforts have become highly visible public relations rollouts with stories on the nightly news. Mom-and-pop businesses, nonprofit organizations, government agencies, educational institutions and all other business entities may at some point face the need to update, redesign or completely rebrand.

For designers—and clients— this can be a terrifying, frustrating and intense process. Designers need to carefully maneuver through the potential landmines of business history and reputation; the "but we've always done things this way" comments; the emotional attachment of clients, employees and customers to an existing identity; the input from those who were not asked; and many other elements that are considered in the process of successfully redesigning the image of a business or organization and reintroducing it to the masses.

Clients, with years of sweat, time and money invested in the public persona of a given business entity, need to remember that some separation anxiety, long nights, floor pacing, and perhaps even a hissy fit or two (from designers and clients) are to be expected as they collaborate to give the company a graphic facelift.

Successful redesign efforts are great collaborations. Design professionals need to bring their knowledge, talent and previous experiences to the project—along with a healthy dose of listening skills, flexibility and humility. Clients should share everything possible about the business in question and be open to the possibility of encountering totally new, unexpected ideas. This is not a time to hoard business secrets. The more information provided to the designer, the better the results. Mutual respect for one another's strengths (and perhaps an occasional acknowledgment of some weaknesses) will help

guide the project to its completion. Both designers and clients should expect some surprises along the way.

Identity Crisis! is not simply a collection of pretty pictures showcasing the identity redesigns of major, recognizable international businesses, although a few such makeovers are briefly highlighted along the way. Instead, this is a volume of redesign and rebranding case studies from design firms of all sizes for clients of all sizes. Creative professionals, from a one-person firm in Portugal to a major player in the Chicago design scene (and entities of all sizes in between), have shared the manner in which they go about dealing with clients and their identity projects. Clients of all types have graciously permitted the presentation of all aspects of the creation of their new business identities.

In compiling this book, it was just as important to present the challenge of introducing a new look for a small neighborhood business as it was to showcase the rebranding of a large nonprofit organization familiar to many. We can all learn from the design challenges and processes of others.

Designers and design students often ask me for one major piece of advice when it comes to the redesign of a business logo. I always respond with "Never tell a potential client that their current logo sucks." In doing so, you can almost guarantee that the client, a family member of the client, or the individual with whom you are dealing played a major role in creating the current image. This seems to hold true whether the client is a one-person home-based business or a large corporation. Making such an insensitive introductory remark is not the best way to start the sometimes long collaborative process of putting the best new face on a client's business or organization.

The book's subtitle, which mentions fifty redesigns, is a bit on the low side. While it's true that only fifty businesses or organizations are showcased in this book, over five hundred images of redesigned corporate identity elements are presented. The projects include redesigned logos, stationery packages, collateral pieces, websites, signage, advertising, magazines, newsletters, vehicle graphics, wearables, packaging and much more.

It is my hope that *Identity Crisis!* will be a valuable resource for designers and clients alike by presenting the "befores," the processes, the "afters," and the successes of redesigns that took somewhat stale business or organization identities to a new and more successful level. The information that a variety of talented design professionals share here may be a primer for other designers taking on the challenge of a redesign. Those on the other side of the project—clients or potential clients—may see that the re-design process isn't necessarily painful, and the results are often incredible.

Jeff Fisher
Engineer of Creative Identity
Jeff Fisher LogoMotives

Identity Crises in Public

In recent years, numerous big corporations have tackled their corporate identity crises in a very open manner. The public seems to be increasingly savvy when it comes to the redesign of highly visible business logos. The attention of the media and the large number of Internet resources has contributed to a greater awareness of redesign and rebranding efforts.

Fortune magazine reporter Telis Demos contacted me after reading my Logo Notions column on the graphic design industry site CreativeLatitude.com. He asked Howard Belk of Siegel+Gale, Bill Gardner of Gardner Design and myself to comment on a variety of logo redesigns that represent major international corporations. Our feedback on the new Kodak, Intel, Sprint and AT&T identities

was featured in the February 6, 2006, print issue of the publication and also online, in the short article, "Logo-Licious or Lame?"

What follows is a brief recap of some recent popular identity redesigns. Hopefully, looking at these recognizable logos will whet your appetite for seeing the real-world solutions offered in the rest of this book.

KODAK IDENTITY REDESIGN

Kodak needed to steer its identity away from the film-related imagery of the past and toward the digital image world of today. Initially, I felt their new image was oversimplified. However, it's growing on me, and I immediately get a mental and visual reference to Kodak when I see the new imagery, due to the use of the same corporate color and similar letterforms within the name. When introduced by the media,

many publications included yellow horizontal lines above and below the new Kodak type treat-

^ Redesigned logo
Kodak logos © 2006 Eastman Kodak Corporation

ment as part of the new image. The official corporate identity does not make use of the line

^ Previous logo

elements. The lack of those lines appears to weaken the strength of the brand identity by eliminating the yellow associated with the Kodak Corporation for so many years. However, this may end up being one of the most successful recent corporate makeovers, thanks to the blanketing of the graphic around the world.

INTEL IDENTITY REDESIGN

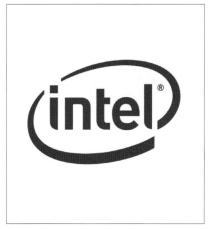

^ Redesigned logo
Intel logos © 2006 Intel Corporation

^ Previous logo

My initial reaction to Intel's new identity was "swoosh-o-licious!" While integrating multiple corporate image elements into a new identity, the inclusion of the swooshes makes the new image seem somewhat dated at introduction. I have a particular aversion to swooshes in logos. They are such a throwback to the "dot-doom" of the 1990s and seem so last century. I'm curious about the timing of the next redesign of this Intel logo.

SPRINT IDENTITY REDESIGN

My initial impression of this design was, "Why is the name so far away from the icon?" In instances where I've seen the logo making use of the icon stacked above the name, the identity seems stronger. I think the identity works as a good combination of the past Sprint and Nextel identities. I look at the word "Sprint" and still see their old red in my mind—while the yellow conveys "Nextel."

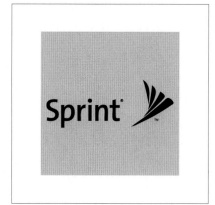

^ Redesigned logo
Sprint and Nextel logos © 2006 Sprint Nextel

^ Previous logos

AT&T IDENTITY REDESIGN

The AT&T rebranding, necessitated by the corporation's association with SBC Communications, is probably my least favorite recent corporate makeover. A classic, easily recognized logo has been altered to look like a marble croquet ball, and the lowercase type of "at&t" looks juvenile. Rather than making the corporation seem more friendly to the world, this design has dumbed down a well-respected graphic image.

˄ Redesigned logo

˄ Previous logos

AT&T and SBC logos © 2006 AT&T Knowledge Ventures

QUARK IDENTITY REDESIGN

The introduction of the former "new" Quark identity redesign had an interesting impact on the design world. Within hours of its introduction, designers around the Internet were finding a variety of incredibly similar logos and posted them on design forums and industry websites.

From the beginning, I thought the icon in the center of the public relations debacle looked more like an *a* rather than a lowercase *q*. It can be very difficult for a designer to create a totally unique image, as this example illustrates on a global level. The newer button-like Quark identity seems to project a much more unique image for the software firm.

˄ Redesigned logo

Quark logos: © 2006 Quark, Inc.

˄ Previous logos

UPS IDENTITY REDESIGN

I still have issues with accepting the new identity UPS introduced in 2003. How dare they mess with Paul Rand's classic logo of my design education?! The new image seems a bit "swooshy" to me, with the arcing line in the upper portion of the design. Initially, in the "Keep It Simple, Stupid" (K.I.S.S.) world of identity design, the three-dimensional treatment of the image generated immediate concerns about the reproduction of such a design. However, I have seen some applications of the logo minus the gradations of the 3-D graphic, and the image does translate well. The design is growing on me, and hopefully the Rand image will continue to be recognized as an example of elegant simplicity as it rests in peace.

⌃ Redesigned logo

⌃ Previous logo

UPS logos: © 2006 United Parcel Service of America, Inc.

UNILEVER IDENTITY REDESIGN

Introduced in 2004, the Unilever logo is one of the best and most unique corporate redesigns in recent years. The logo is beautiful, fun to dissect and somehow—even with all its detail—works well in very small applications. The new symbol also eliminates the World Trade Center tower imagery of the old design—a major concern following 9/11. The new identity gives this large corporation a great deal of personality.

⌃ Redesigned logo

⌃ Previous logo

Unilever logos: © 2006 Unilever PLC/Unilever N.V.

USA NETWORK IDENTITY REDESIGN

It is interesting that the USA Network opted to eliminate the American flag imagery in its most recent logo design, in these patriotic times. The television entity was introduced in 1980 with a simple red, white and blue type treatment. A star was incorporated into the design in 1996 and the traditional colors were dropped. The flag imagery originally appeared in 1999—with red, white and blue implemented again—and the flowing flag was then streamlined in 2002. While the new flagless design of October 2005 is a simpler and stronger treatment of the USA imagery, I do snicker a bit at what appears to me to be male genitalia coming off of the *U* and *A* letterforms in the logo. After I point it out to people, they say it's all they see each time the logo appears on the television screen. Once again, the patriotic colors have surprisingly disappeared.

^ Redesigned logo

USA Network logos: © 2006 NBC Universal, Inc.

^ Previous logos

VISA IDENTITY REDESIGN

^ Redesigned logo

Visa logos: © 2006 Visa U.S.A. and Visa International Service Association

^ Previous logos

This rebranding, an attempt to coordinate all Visa's identity imagery worldwide, works very well for me. The change was so subtle I doubt if many customers have even noticed. The graphic has been cleaned up and simplified. In the end, there is no doubt that it still says "Visa."

IDENTITY
REDESIGNS

ANNE *Pettygrove*
CHIEF ADMINISTRATIVE OFFICER

Women helping women reach for the stars.

P.E.O.*Executive Office* DES MOINES, *Iowa* *Phone:* 515.255.7437

3700 *Grand Avenue* 50312.2899 *Fax:* 515.255.3820

WWW.PEOINTERNATIONAL.ORG

ANNE *Pettygrove*

CHIEF ADMINISTRATIVE OFFICER

P.E.O.*Executive Office*
3700 *Grand Avenue*
DES MOINES, *Iowa* 50312.2899

Phone: 515.255.7437
Fax: 515.255.3820
CAO@PEODSM.ORG

WWW.PEOINTERNATIONAL.ORG

P.E.O. *Executive Office* DES MOINES, *Iowa*

3700 *Grand Avenue* 50312.2899

Women helping women reach for the stars.

Women helping women reach for the stars.

P.E.O. International Sisterhood

PROJECT:

P.E.O. International Sisterhood identity

DESIGN FIRM:

Sayles Graphic Design

LOCATION:

Des Moines, Iowa

ART DIRECTOR/DESIGNER:

John Sayles

COPYWRITERS:

Sheree Clark, Wendy Lyons

When P.E.O. began in 1869, it was a college sorority. During this era, keeping "secrets" was a common way to create bonds of friendship. Today, the Iowa-based organization boasts a membership of more than 250,000 women. While members continue to honor the founders by keeping the literal meaning of P.E.O. private, the group had been exploring the idea that it was too quiet about its great work. A philanthropic organization, P.E.O. helps women achieve educational goals by providing grants, scholarships, awards and loans.

In late 2003, the executive board authorized a complete image overhaul to be led by Sayles Graphic Design. Eschewing publicity and public recognition, P.E.O. deliberately stayed out of the spotlight for 137 years. Because a more proactive publicity policy would be such a major shift in the organization's culture, an internal communications campaign was necessary.

During the course of planning meetings with Sayles staff, a phrase kept coming up as the group discussed ways for the

^ Redesigned logo

<<Redesigned letterhead, envelope and business card

^ Previous logo

The cover image contains:

THE RECORD | PERIODICAL

SEPTEMBER · OCTOBER 2005

SPREAD THE WORD! PAGE 23

IT'S OK — TO — TALK — ABOUT — P.E.O.

Women helping women reach for the stars.

⌃ Redesigned publication cover

organization to grow and prosper in the future. The group agreed that "It's OK to Talk About P.E.O." could work as a theme for the internal communications campaign.

Sayles suggested the program kick off with a "teaser" campaign in *The P.E.O. Record*—the official magazine of the Sisterhood—as a first step. The message of this initial phase of the promotion was simply "It's OK." Designer John Sayles treated the "It's OK" message as a graphic, placing it in a circle, and—to add visual appeal and intrigue to the ads—included portraits of P.E.O.'s seven founders. Because the portraits were already familiar to members, this approach gave the impression that the OK message was actually something that the original seven would endorse.

Upon arrival at the 2005 International Convention of the P.E.O. Sisterhood, delegates and guests were exposed to even more "It's OK" messages. From hotel room key holders to artfully placed signs and even little mint candies, the idea that "It's OK" appeared to be everywhere. The inescapable messages had the desired effect of creating a substantial curiosity among the delegates.

The "It's OK to Talk About P.E.O." campaign was designed to preview the new P.E.O. corporate identity without actually revealing it. The color palette of magenta, lime and yellow created for the teaser program was also the color scheme for the permanent identity. The graphic flower that punctuated the new P.E.O. logo is the same one that appeared inside the O of "OK." This approach had many positive features, including a visual continuity that ran from the teaser campaign to the introduction of the new corporate identity.

Redesigned brochure cover

WHAT'S OK?

EVERYTHING YOU WANTED TO TELL YOUR FRIENDS ABOUT P.E.O. BUT WERE AFRAID TO!

P.E.O. was founded in 1869 as a college sorority – a secret sisterhood of young girls who were passionate about women's education. During this era, keeping girlish "secrets" was a common way to create bonds of friendship. Even after P.E.O. evolved into a community organization, we continued to honor the tradition of keeping the true meaning of our letters to ourselves. Not because we desire to be a "clandestine group" – but because it's our way of paying homage to P.E.O.'s founding sisters and their youthful zeal.

Today, P.E.O. enters a new era. While we hold fast to our pledge to not utter the "true" meaning of the letters in public, the mission that our name stands for is one that deserves to be shouted from the rooftops. This guide will help you understand what we mean when we say "It's ok to talk about P.E.O."

HERE'S WHAT P.E.O. SISTERS DO:

- Say we are a "Philanthropic Educational Organization."
- Share our mission statement.
- Share our tagline.
- Use the logo: Both the historic "star" version and the newer stylized one on this brochure.
- Print P.E.O. T-shirts and wear them with pride.
- Put P.E.O. on your resume.
- Wear our emblem (or P.E.O. recognition pin) proudly, even on non-meeting days!
- Talk every day about P.E.O.
- Refer your friends to the P.E.O. Website! There's lots of information there for the general public to read.

HERE'S WHAT P.E.O. SISTERS DON'T DO:

- Tell the true meaning of our letters or our password. *Share our tagline or mission statement instead. If asked about the REAL meaning, explain that it is a P.E.O. tradition to honor our Founders – young Victorian girls who enjoyed keeping "girlhood secrets" – by keeping the meaning of our letters to themselves.*

PLEASE SHARE WITH EVERYONE WHAT P.E.O. IS:

- An international women's organization with a tradition of friendship that spans nearly 140 years.
- A healthy, growing organization – our membership is increasing.
- A positive force in the community with our projects helping women reach their educational goals.
- Proud of our heritage of providing over $147 million in educational financial assistance for more than 73,000 women.
- The steward of Cottey College, an educational institution from which more than 7,500 women have graduated.
- A group that serves women worldwide.
- A diverse sisterhood that welcomes women of all races, religions and backgrounds.
- *Women helping women reach for the stars.*

P.E.O. IS NOT:

- A "secret" organization. While the password and true meaning of our letters is "kept private," our mission is not. Please, don't refer to our sisterhood as "secret."
- An elitist group. We welcome all women who demonstrate a passion for our mission.
- Interested in superseding any individual's personal interests or beliefs.

Women helping women reach for the stars.

P·E·O

Redesigned brochure interior

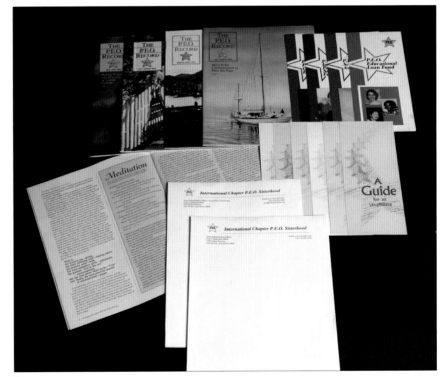

Previous stationery package, publications and collateral materials

Toppers Pizza

PROJECT:
Toppers Pizza—Feed the Need redesign

DESIGN FIRM:
Shine Advertising Co.

LOCATION:
Madison, Wisconsin

CREATIVE DIRECTOR:
Mike Kriefski

ART DIRECTOR:
John Krull

COPYWRITER:
James Breen

ILLUSTRATOR:
Nate Williams

Over the past decade, the pizza category has become a sea of sameness, with each major player trying to be all things to all people. Enter Toppers Pizza, a regional pizza chain with a bold new campaign from Shine Advertising. A campaign with a singular focus: own the college market.

"We saw Toppers as a prime example of what the pizza industry has become. No real and meaningful difference was seen, but the potential for something so much more was there," said John Krull, associate creative director for Shine Advertising. "Once we narrowed our focus to the college

^ Redesigned logo
<< Redesigned pizza boxes

^ Previous logos

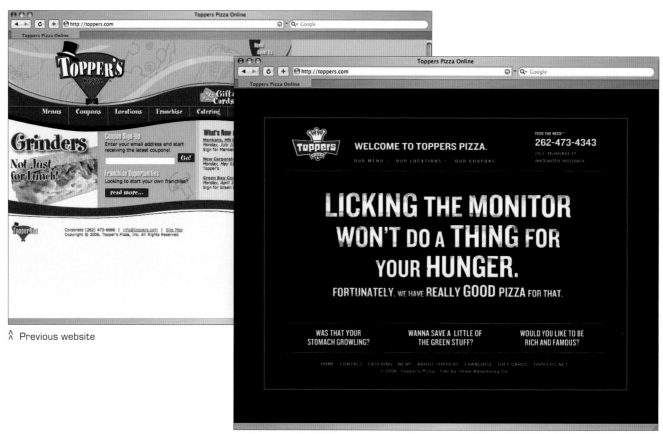

∧ Previous website

∧ Redesigned website

∧ Redesigned restaurant menu

∧ Previous menu

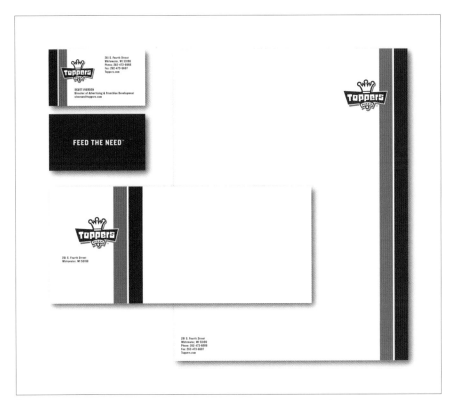

‸ Redesigned business card (front and back), envelope and letterhead

‸ Previous business card

‸ Redesigned staff uniforms

‸ Previous staff uniforms

market, our job became incredibly simple and incredibly exciting—create breakthrough work that puts a stake in the ground."

With a mission to unite Toppers with college students, Shine Advertising took an unconventional approach at every point of contact. It started with a new logo, embellished with a crown, and the tagline "Feed the Need." From there, print ads with headlines like "Every Pizza Is Made With Tender Loving Care. The Exact Same Way We Treated Your Girlfriend Last Night" and mechanic shirt uniforms emblazoned with the new logo were born. Direct mail sent to college students included not just a menu but foldout posters with outlandish illustrations by Nate Williams and irreverent narratives about conquering hunger. Launching in early September 2006, the new campaign clearly establishes Toppers Pizza as the one and only pizza brand for the college market.

ADIGE · Veicoli Industriali

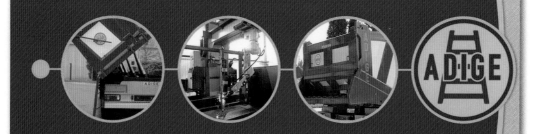

Una continua innovazione. Dal 1919.

Adige

PROJECT:
Adige corporate identity update

DESIGN FIRM:
Studio GT&P

LOCATION:
Foligno, Italy

CREATIVE DIRECTOR/DESIGNER:
Gianluigi Tobanelli

Adige was one of the first Italian companies in the business of constructing semitrailers. It has been one of the leaders in the industry since the early years of the twentieth century. However, the business had not paid much attention to visual communica-tion or business image over the years.

In 2005, Adige felt it neces-sary to update the company's corporate identity—without giv-ing up the old, recognized firm logo. Gianluigi Tobanelli, of Studio GT&P, improved upon the old design simply by using of a new font to improve the readability of the company name. The designer also made slight adjustments to various graphic elements within the identity and defined a new corporate color palette.

∧ Redesigned promotional brochure interior
<< Redesigned promotional brochure cover

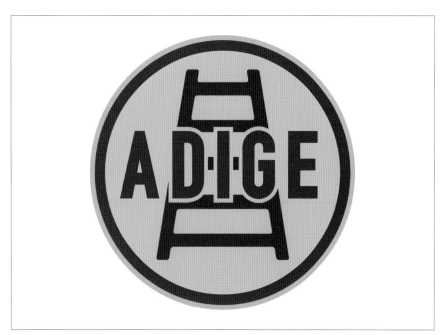

∧ Redesigned logo

∧ Previous logo

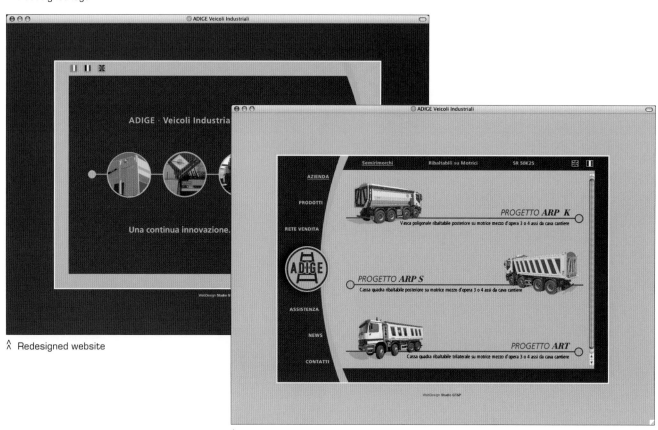

∧ Redesigned website

∧ Redesigned website

^ Redesigned promotional flyer

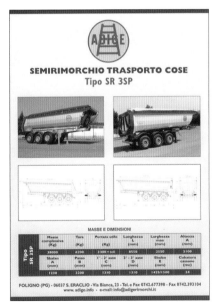

^ Previous promotional flyer

^ Redesigned stationery package

Richard A. Maranto
President

8064 Geaslin Drive
Middletown, MD 21769

301.371.4422 Phone
301.676.9918 Mobile
rich@ram-digital.com

www.ram-digital.com

RAMDigital

NEW MEDIA DEVELOPMENT

RAMDigital

NEW MEDIA DEVELOPMENT

www.ram-digital.com

301.676.9918 Mobile

301.371.4422 Phone

8064 Geaslin Drive, Middletown, MD 21769

RAMDigital | 8064 Geaslin Drive
Middletown, MD 21769

NEW MEDIA DEVELOPMENT

RAM Digital

PROJECT:
RAM Digital logo redesign

DESIGN FIRM:
Octavo Designs

LOCATION:
Frederick, Maryland

ART DIRECTOR:
Sue Hough

DESIGNERS:
Mark Burrier, Sue Hough

RAM Digital came to Octavo Designs for a fresh approach in their business identity. The company's previous logo was designed quickly in house and the company was never quite satisfied with it as a trademark.

"We were allowed free reign to play with any concepts, visuals and colors. This was rebuilding from the ground up," said Sue Hough, art director on the project.

RAM Digital develops traditional multimedia and innovative web applications, so they need to look like a new media company. The new design shows an interlocking shape that grows, which is a reference to technology/multimedia growing beyond conventions. The interlocking shape wraps around a circle, which implies that it creates a perfect solution. The typeface Preface was used for its clarity and boldness.

RAM Digital

∧ Redesigned logo
<< Redesigned business card, letterhead (front and back) and envelope

RAM digital ⠿.

∧ Previous logo

BRENTWOOD CLASSICS

KIMBERLEY SELDON for BRENTWOOD CLASSICS

BRENTWOOD CLASSICS

For those who studied our Classics,
here's something new...

Pour ceux qui ont étudié nos classiques,
voici quelque chose de nouveau.

BRENTWOOD CLASSICS

For those who studied our Classics,
here's something new...

WEB & COIL

CLIENT IN CRISIS

Brentwood Classics

PROJECT:
Brentwood Classics identity

DESIGN FIRM:
3 Dogz Creative Inc.

LOCATION:
Toronto, Ontario, Canada

ART DIRECTORS:
Dave Gouveia, Chris Elkerton, Roberta Judge

DESIGNER:
Ryan Broadbent

Celebrating over thirty-five years in the furniture industry, Brentwood Classics' secret to success is facilitating consumer demands and understanding market trends. A family-owned and -operated business, well recognized in the furniture industry with numerous Canadian Home Furnishings awards, Brentwood nevertheless felt it was time for change.

Furniture styles were beginning to move away from traditional into the realm of contemporary. At the suggestion of PR consultant Irene Carroll, Brentwood had decided to partner with well-known Interior Designer Kimberley Seldon to develop a signature line.

Carroll approached 3 Dogz Creative about revising the Brentwood Classics identity. Given the high profile of the Kimberley Seldon Design Group, 3 Dogz Creative saw an opportunity to rebrand Brentwood, along with the launch of the signature line.

The existing logo was dated and in need of a fresh look to bring the company into the here and now. The new identity also had to promote Brentwood Classics as an individual company, yet be flexible enough to integrate Seldon's existing brand for the cross promotion.

The logo redevelopment was a difficult process given that the previous logo had been around for so long, and owner, Guy Sisto, feared drastic change would alienate

BRENTWOOD CLASSICS

ꞈ Previous logo

ꞈ Redesigned logo
<< Redesigned collateral

27

∧ Redesigned stationery package

older existing customers. However, Sisto's two daughters, Cindy and Diana (both involved in all company dealings), were included in every meeting, and their youthful energy and eagerness to push for change helped support design arguments.

The final result was a stripped-down version of the basics of furniture making. Two frames, side by side, represented the building blocks that were essential to the production of every piece of furniture in the warehouse. An ani-

mated version of these blocks was later introduced on the website, show casing how these two frames could easily be the start of any piece of furniture. A simplified typographic treatment was utilized, eliminating much of the earlier "fluff," such as the tagline, and the red color was abandoned for a dark gray and cool blue tones.

The new look then spilled into all facets of the company: stationery, furniture tags, a press kit, catalogs, labels, the website and more. The interior showroom was revamped to showcase Brentwood Classics' award-winning furniture, and a release party was held to promote the Kimberley Seldon signature line.

The results: Brentwood Classics' sales have been steadily increasing since the rebrand, and 3 Dogz Creative continues to work closely with this client.

WORDS OF WISDOM

"Most identity projects are actually brand strategy or positioning projects in disguise. In your first conversation with the prospective client, ask them to produce written documentation of their positioning statement, values and key attributes. If they can't, you're likely dealing with a company that doesn't have a clear definition of its brand—and your proposal should include a strategy phase.

Oftentimes, the most challenging aspect of large identity assignments isn't the creative, it's establishing clear decision-making criteria and creating consensus within the management team and other key constituents.

Do your homework. Learn everything you can (industry, competition, audience) about the company/business you are designing for. Before you begin any creative explorations, be sure you have defined and approved decision-making criteria agreed upon by the client. Without this, you may find your final work being judged by the CEO's spouse.

In the creative exploration phase, capture every idea, even those early ones you think aren't going anywhere. Resist the temptation to refine too early.

When reviewing your final options, ask yourself if it is something that meets the criteria you've established, and if it will still be relevant twenty years from now.

A trendy typeface is not a substitute for a good idea."

Bob Domenz
Avenue Marketing & Communications
Chicago, Illinois
www.avenue-inc.com

http://www.sharedownershiphomes.org/

Google

Shared Ownership: Helping people with disabilities pur...

 Page ▾ Tools ▾

Change text size: ➕ ➖

Helping people with learning disabilities purchase a home of their own

Shared Ownership Homes has teamed up with a number of major Housing Associations, Care Providers, Charities and Lenders to help people with learning disabilities enjoy the benefits of home ownership. **Find out more...**

Home

The Problem

Shared Ownership

Our Partners

How It Works

Do I Qualify?

About Us

Contact Us

Professional Advisors

Now you really can be a home owner. Here are the key benefits:

- ■ You can buy a home up to the value of £200,000
- ■ Your home will be owned jointly by you and a Housing Association
- ■ Your half will be purchased with a mortgage which will be arranged for you without cost
- ■ You will pay NO fees to buy your home
- ■ You will pay NO mortgage or rent - they are covered by State Benefits

What's the problem?
Lorem ipsum dolor sit amet consectetuer adipiscing elit euismod tincidunt ut lacreet dolore magna volutpat.
More...

What's the solution?
Lorem ipsum dolor sit amet consectetuer adipiscing elit euismod tincidunt ut lacreet dolore magna volutpat.
More...

Do I qualify?
Lorem ipsum dolor sit amet consectetuer adipiscing elit euismod tincidunt ut lacreet dolore magna volutpat.
More...

What's life like for people with a learning disability?
Find out with Mencap's interactive quiz about understanding learning disability. **Start the quiz...**

Internet   100%

Shared Ownership Homes

PROJECT:

Shared Ownership Homes
identity and website

DESIGN FIRM:

Common Sense Design

LOCATION:

New Hamburg, Ontario, Canada

ART DIRECTOR/DESIGNER:

Nigel Gordijk

The UK-based charitable organization Shared Ownership Homes (SOH) has teamed up with a number of major housing associations, care providers, charities and lenders to help people with disabilities enjoy the benefits of home ownership. The original version of SOH's website and logo needed an update to coincide with a major marketing push in 2006.

The previous brand used bold colors that helped make it distinctive, but they needed to be implemented with more consideration. The old logo featured two semicircles to symbolize the act of sharing but didn't illustrate the home ownership part of SOH's work.

Issues of website usability and accessibility also needed to be addressed in anticipation of the site reaching a larger audience. The wide measure of the text made it difficult to read because readers would get to the end of one line and then struggle to find the start of the next. Small inset photos of disabled people showed the target market for the agency services at a glance. However, the pictures were small, so the web pages looked unfriendly because they were copy heavy.

British-born Nigel Gordijk of Common Sense Design was commissioned by SOH to create a

^ Redesigned logo
<<Redesigned website

^ Previous logo

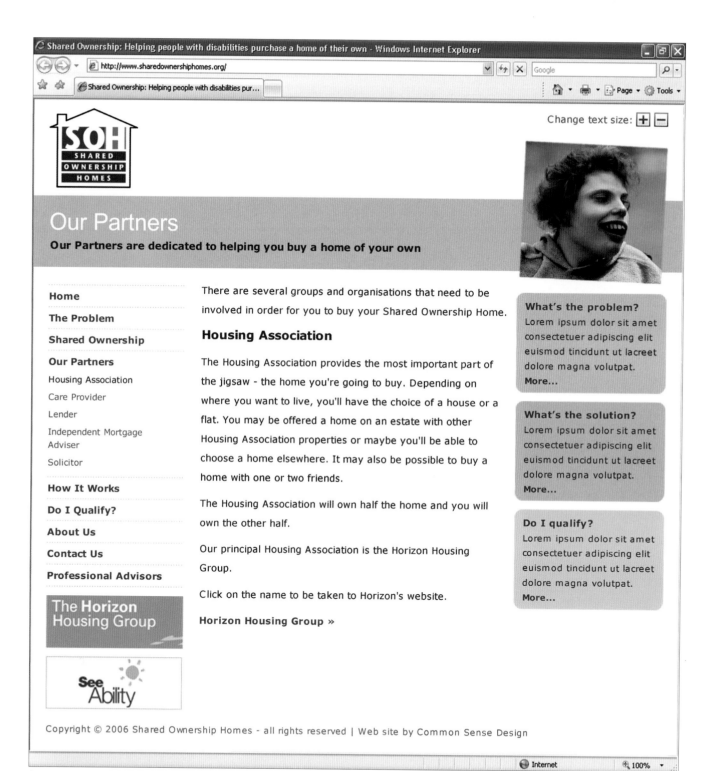

Shared Ownership: Helping people with disabilities purchase a home of their own - Windows Internet Explorer

http://www.sharedownershiphomes.org/

Google

Shared Ownership: Helping people with disabilities pur...

Page ▾ | Tools ▾

Change text size: + −

Our Partners

Our Partners are dedicated to helping you buy a home of your own

Home

The Problem

Shared Ownership

Our Partners

Housing Association

Care Provider

Lender

Independent Mortgage Adviser

Solicitor

How It Works

Do I Qualify?

About Us

Contact Us

Professional Advisors

The **Horizon** Housing Group

See Ability

There are several groups and organisations that need to be involved in order for you to buy your Shared Ownership Home.

Housing Association

The Housing Association provides the most important part of the jigsaw - the home you're going to buy. Depending on where you want to live, you'll have the choice of a house or a flat. You may be offered a home on an estate with other Housing Association properties or maybe you'll be able to choose a home elsewhere. It may also be possible to buy a home with one or two friends.

The Housing Association will own half the home and you will own the other half.

Our principal Housing Association is the Horizon Housing Group.

Click on the name to be taken to Horizon's website.

Horizon Housing Group »

What's the problem?
Lorem ipsum dolor sit amet consectetuer adipiscing elit euismod tincidunt ut lacreet dolore magna volutpat.
More...

What's the solution?
Lorem ipsum dolor sit amet consectetuer adipiscing elit euismod tincidunt ut lacreet dolore magna volutpat.
More...

Do I qualify?
Lorem ipsum dolor sit amet consectetuer adipiscing elit euismod tincidunt ut lacreet dolore magna volutpat.
More...

Copyright © 2006 Shared Ownership Homes - all rights reserved | Web site by Common Sense Design

Internet   100%

∧ Previous website

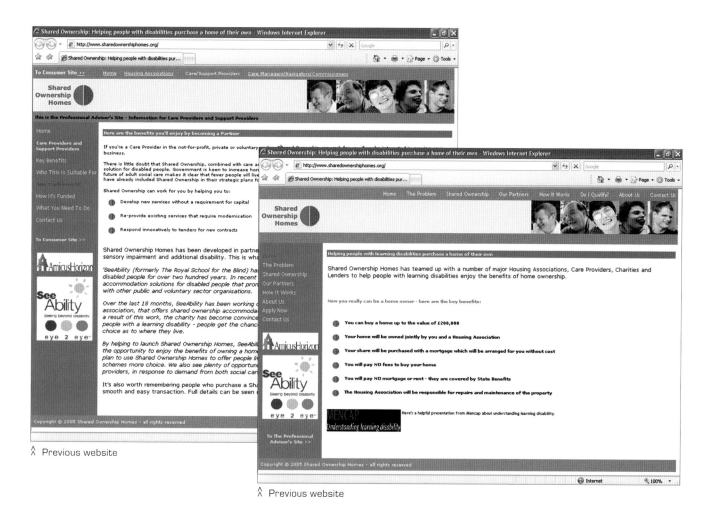

^ Previous website

^ Previous website

modern and professional image. Nigel decided to stick with the same color palette in order to retain an element of familiarity. The logo now has a simple house shape that contains the organization's name and its initials in three colored blocks.

The original logo's three colors are still evident on the new site design but are used more sparingly. More white space and larger photographs contribute to a more open look and feel. Infor-mation is presented in a narrower, fixed width that makes it easier to read. Colored text is reserved for links only, so that they stand out and their function is obvious (previously, some subheadings were also in color).

The result is a more consistent, integrated brand and a friend-lier, engaging web presence. The navigation and page layouts are easier to use, so the site has better accessibility, which is vital for disabled people who make up the target audience. Buttons in the top right of every page enable visitors to easily and intuitively increase and decrease the size of the screen fonts.

A sister site for professionals provides useful information for organizations that want to play a part in this venture. The website uses other hues from the same palette to help differentiate it from the consumer version.

ATLAS
ECONOMIC RESEARCH FOUNDATION

2000 N. 14TH STREET • SUITE 550 • ARLINGTON, VA 22201
TEL 703 934 6969• WWW.ATLASUSA.ORG • ATLAS@ATLASUSA.ORG

ATLAS
ECONOMIC RESEARCH FOUNDATION

ALEJANDRO A. CHAFUEN, PH.D.
PRESIDENT & CEO

2000 N. 14TH STREET
SUITE 550
ARLINGTON, VA 22201
TEL 703 934 6969
WWW.ATLASUSA.ORG
ALEX.CHAFUEN@ATLASUSA.ORG

ATLAS
ECONOMIC RESEARCH FOUNDATION

2000 N. 14TH STREET • SUITE 550 • ARLINGTON, VA 2220

Atlas Economic Research Foundation

PROJECT:
Atlas Economic Research Foundation identity redesign

DESIGN FIRM:
CC Graphic Design

LOCATION:
Salt Lake City, Utah

CREATIVE DIRECTOR/DESIGNER:
Carolyn Crowley

Atlas Economic Research Foundation is a nonprofit organization that focuses on bringing freedom to the world by helping develop and strengthen a global network of market-oriented think tanks. The ideas the organization wanted to communicate through its image included global reach, a promoter of truth and good scholarship, and a champion of individual rights and economic freedom. In addition, the organization is growing and wanted a new look that would represent new ideas and future growth. The previous logo and identity did not have a consistent look and featured poorly drawn line art of a globe, a book, and an *A*, none of which successfully communicated these ideas.

The idea for the new logo and identity was to create a world based on dots representing the international, worldly connections Atlas makes every day. In addition, the dots give the world a mosaic look, which contributes to Atlas's image of international reach and all types of people coming together from different backgrounds. The organization wanted to keep some type of reference to the old logo so that their clients would be

^ Redesigned logo
<<Redesigned business card, letterhead and envelope

^ New 25th anniversary logo

^ Previous logo

able to identify them. To achieve this, Crowley included the lines of a globe and put typographic focus on the *A* in *Atlas*, similar to the client's old logo. In addition, the *A* and *T* hold up the globe as a reference to the mythological figure, Atlas, holding up the world on his shoulders. The designer created the logo in two colors to keep the cost of printed materials down. Red and blue represent the academic and scholarly side of Atlas, while the Copperplate Gothic font presents a classic yet streamlined look.

Once the logo was approved, Crowley applied this design approach to the client's overall identity, including letterhead, business cards, envelopes and notepads.

⌃ Redesigned 25th anniversary letterhead

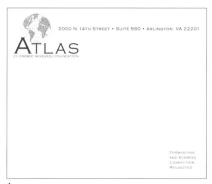

⌃ Redesigned stickers

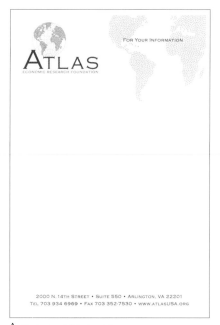

⌃ Redesigned notepad

ʌ Redesigned logo on office window

ʌ Redesigned badge template

ʌ Redesigned catalog envelope

WORDS OF WISDOM

"Don't start designing until you are clear, and your client is clear, on their design goals as leaders."

Tony Spaeth
Identityworks
Rye, New York
www.identityworks.com

**FAGERHOLM &
JEFFERSON**
Law Corporation

> 3500 W. Olive Avenue,
Third Floor
Burbank, CA 91505

> Tel: 818.973.2731
> Fax: 818.973.2734
> info@fjlawcorp.com

> www.fjlawcorp.com

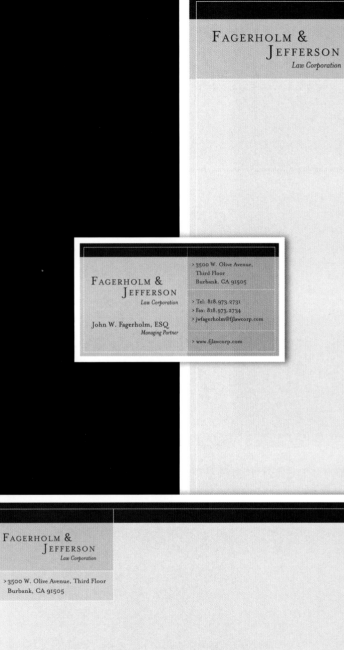

**FAGERHOLM &
JEFFERSON**
Law Corporation

John W. Fagerholm, ESQ
Managing Partner

> 3500 W. Olive Avenue,
Third Floor
Burbank, CA 91505

> Tel: 818.973.2731
> Fax: 818.973.2734
> jwfagerholm@fjlawcorp.com

> www.fjlawcorp.com

**FAGERHOLM &
JEFFERSON**
Law Corporation

>3500 W. Olive Avenue, Third Floor
Burbank, CA 91505

Fagerholm & Jefferson Law Corporation

PROJECT:
Fagerholm & Jefferson Law Corporation identity

DESIGN FIRM:
Mayhem Studios

LOCATION:
Los Angeles, California

CREATIVE DIRECTOR/DESIGNER:
Calvin Lee

The Fagerholm & Jefferson Law Corporation approached Mayhem Studios for help in developing the company's identity and brand recognition. It wanted to be recognized as a well-established law firm.

The challenge was to create a conservative, yet not boring, identity for Fagerholm & Jefferson, allowing them to stand out from other law firms. Mayhem Studios began the project with a nearly clean slate, as a strong identity did not previously exist. The previous identity was simply the firm name in Helvetica, centered in a white field, on all stationery elements. The company didn't have a website at the time.

The challenge in designing a mark for a law firm is to be professional in presenting a legal entity without being clichéd. Mayhem Studios opted to make use of a type treatment rather than incorporating graphic illustrative elements. The designer used a clean, classy font; a grid system with strong structure and lines; and a color palette of browns, tans and earth tones. The end product conveys a strong, solid company people can trust.

John W. Fagerholm, of Fagerholm & Jefferson Law Corporation, gives Mayhem Studios high praise:

"Thanks so much for the great work. My business cards and website are fabulous. I would have never thought to use those colors

^ Redesigned logo
<< Redesigned business card, letterhead and envelope

FAGERHOLM & JEFFERSON
Law Corporation

^ Previous logo

∧ Previous business card

∧ Redesigned website page

in that combination. I have had so many great compliments on my cards. I appreciate the time you took to listen to what I needed and figure out the solution. In the past, I have not been able to find business cards that were professional enough to say 'I can handle whatever you throw at me' but at the same time say 'I'm hip enough to be practicing entertainment law.' You found the right combination. Thanks again. People I know will be calling you."

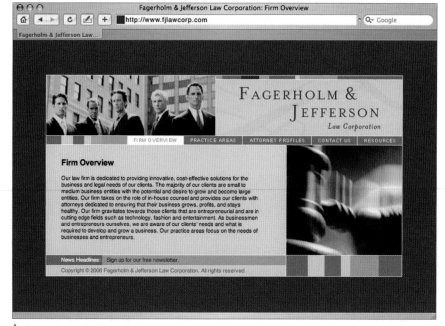

∧ Redesigned website page

WORDS OF WISDOM

"According to many dictionaries, the word *change* means the following: to cause to be different or to give a completely different form or appearance, to transform. But more often than not, change within an organization is seen as risky and a threat to security.

Research suggests that people will actively fight or resist any new direction in their work environment unless they are convinced that this change will benefit the entire work team. I have discovered that people don't fear actual changes, what they fear is a loss of security with any new environment.

Almost synonymous with the fear of change is the fear of failure. Many people feel worried and anxious when they consider undertaking anything new for fear of making a mistake. This fear is so overwhelming that any change at all will create a sense of dread and pessimism.

Oscar Wilde once said, 'Consistency is the last refuge of the unimaginative.' What is most fortunate for folks working with corporate identity is that the surest way to impact unimaginative people is to help them *discover* their imagination. Creativity is one of the most inspiring ways to indicate and announce change. It is hard work, but ultimately, with the right skills, the power of positive creativity can inspire the most fearful of clients."

Debbie Millman
Sterling Brands
New York City, New York
www.debbiemillman.com

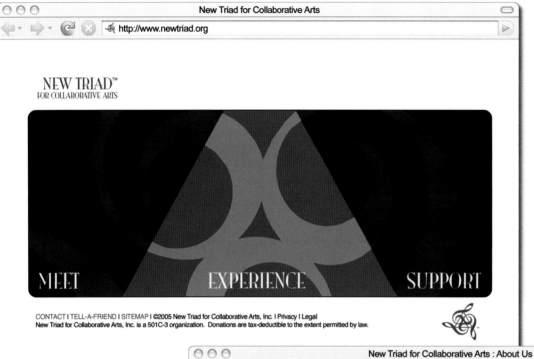

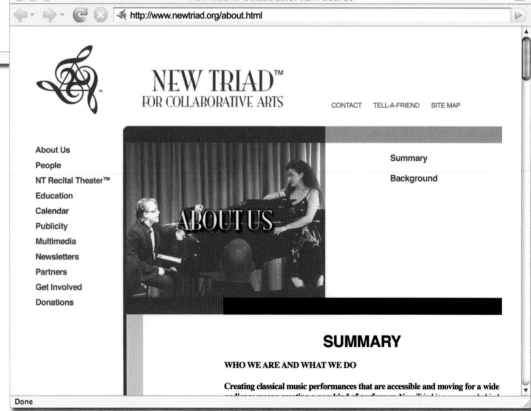

New Triad for Collaborative Arts

PROJECT:
New Triad website redesign and brand extension

DESIGN FIRM:
Finamore Design

LOCATION:
Brooklyn, New York

CREATIVE DIRECTOR:
Troy Finamore

New Triad is an educational, nonprofit organization that is passionately committed to revolutionizing song recitals through the power of collaboration. The client had recently increased the number of classes and performances offered and was looking to solicit donations to help fund this growth.

Their original website was built using a flash-based template. The website did not reflect the organization's brand image, most of the content was outdated, and the website was not generating the kind of interest or traffic the client was seeking.

Discussions with the client established the following goals for the redesign of the website:

- incorporate the client's logo and identity
- make use of clear and consistent navigation, and logical content flow
- create a safe avenue for accepting donations
- enable easy website updates

Λ Redesigned logo
<< Redesigned website

Λ Previous website

The new website design complements New Triad's identity, and the website is now a useful communications tool. After completion of the website, Finamore Design went on to develop templates for both newsletters and promotional DVDs. The client now proudly directs users to the new website, and the number of students and supporters continues to grow.

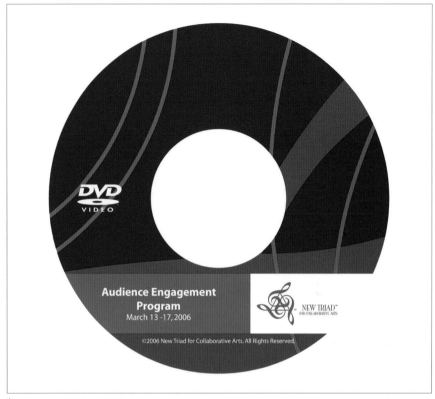

⌃ Redesigned logo on DVD

⌃ Redesigned logo on DVD jacket

NEW TRIAD™
FOR COLLABORATIVE ARTS

July 2006, Volume 2, No. 2

*Our Mission is to pioneer a new theatrical format
for classical music recitals that fully engages audiences.*

MESSAGE FROM THE FOUNDER

BREAKTHROUGH

Dear Friends of New Triad,

How many people are lucky enough to witness the moment a caterpillar turns into a butterfly and to watch it take wing? This is what an overflowing and enthusiastic audience experienced on March 17th at the Yamaha Piano Salon in Manhattan at the showcase performance of New Triad's first foray into training instrumentalists as well as the singer-pianist teams for which it has become well known.

For years the classical music world has been valiantly working at new ways to entice audiences to its concerts. Some vocal recital organizations favor supertitles, many performances feature multi-media projections of evocative images and almost every organization sends out a battalion of outreach programs to stave off the cuts in arts funding in the schools.

All of these efforts are worthy. But are they really drawing new audiences to classical music? Are they really getting at the essence of what is lacking? Is classical music in our times bound to be a caterpillar inching along the ground never to experience transformation?

Four years ago, New Triad came into existence because its eventual founders were asking hard questions about what was turning audiences away. Granted, we were no longer a country full of first-generation Americans whose parents brought classical culture with them from Europe. Given that, we knew it was important to look to ourselves for answers. We had discussed how the overemphasis both on technical perfection and on the overly self-absorbed personas classical musicians have traditionally been encouraged to adopt were at odds with the public's clear desire

for a closer identification with the performing experience, as evidenced today by the popularity of such reality shows as *American Idol*.

While keeping the integrity of the art intact, New Triad is working to transform the very essence of performing relationships; to help artists relate more personally to their art, to form more mutually supportive musical partnerships and to strive towards a natural, vital connection with audiences from the moment they enter the theater.

The butterflies that emerged on March 17th at the Yamaha Piano salon in New York were the lovely result of the way in which each of the three already outstanding musical artists took their music to a more meaningful level by defining for themselves and for their audience what the pieces meant to them on a profoundly personal level. Performing with a greater sense of ease and humanity, often these artists expressed their feelings in words, at other times in gestures and movement and sometimes in the timing of the silences.

Their New Triad training included a wide variety of courses such as *Introduction to New Triad, Speaking with Your Audience, Communicative Mastery, Dynamics of Collaboration, Dramatic Analysis and Interpretation, Connecting Through Body Awareness* and *Dramatic Presentation*. The shift in intent was evident to those in attendance after having watched a short piece at the beginning of the recital of moments filmed earlier that same week prior to any training with the extraordinary New Triad faculty.

Thank you Julia Mintzer, soprano, Stefan Milenkovich, violinist and Konstantin Soukhovetski, pianist, for helping us inaugurate this new phase of New Triad's development.

With great excitement,

*Dr. Arlene Shrut
Founder and Artistic Director*

Julia Mintzer, soprano

Konstantin Soukhovetski, pianist

Stefan Milenkovich, violinist

**www.newtriad.org
(for calendar events}**

Ʌ Redesigned newsletter

http://vanderveercenter.com/

VanderVeer Center

The Art & Science of Image Enhancement®

Home • Our Team • Services • Videos • Specials • Contact Us

Medical Services

- The VanderVeer Lift®
- Non-Surgical Facelift
- I2PL Photo Rejuvenation
- Laser Hair Removal
- BOTOX® Cosmetic
- Dermal Fillers
- Medical Microdermabrasion
- Medical Peels
- Mesotherapy for Face
- Mesotherapy for Body
- Mesotherapy for Cellulite
- MesoLift - MesoGlow
- Sclerotherapy
- Acne Action Plan[SM]
- Wellness Supplements
- Skin Care & Products

Art

Dr. Elizabeth VanderVeer with her own painting, "In a Figurative Light."

Artist

Elizabeth VanderVeer, M.D.
Board Certified Physician
Owner and Medical Director

Canvas

Put *your* canvas in the hands of *this* artist

Done

VanderVeer Center

PROJECT:
VanderVeer Center
brand redesign

DESIGN FIRM:
Jeff Fisher LogoMotives

LOCATION:
Portland, Oregon

CREATIVE DIRECTOR/DESIGNER:
Jeff Fisher

With the use of a couple of different names and major personnel changes in the course of several months, the organization that was to become the VanderVeer Center was going though a major identity crisis. The one constant in the process was Dr. Elizabeth VanderVeer. With the latest changes and the business taking on her name, she came to my design firm at the suggestion of her husband, a former Logomotives client.

The facility, specializing in non-surgical cosmetic procedures, wanted to attract a high-end clientele from throughout the Portland metropolitan area, the Pacific Northwest and beyond. However, the identity and past promotion efforts had not conveyed a high-end image. In fact, at one point in the design process, the designer likened some previous advertising designs to those of an auto body repair shop.

In interviewing Dr. VanderVeer, I discovered that she was also an artist and had a passion for European travel and culture. That information led to the my suggestion of the tagline "The Art & Science of Image Enhancement." The use of the words "art," "artist" and

‸ Redesigned logo
<< VanderVeer Center website

Nūlife
Aesthetic Wellness Centers

‸ Previous logo prior to company
name change

△ Redesigned print ad

△ Previous print ad prior to name change

△ Previous print ad prior to name change

"canvas" were to be incorporated as branding elements in all marketing and promotional items to reinforce the creative aspect of the doctor's work. It was determined that Tuscan colors would be used to convey a rich old world feeling.

From that message evolved the look and feel of the new logo, corporate colors and branding image. The design elements quickly came together with the photography of Loma Smith in the creation of the first major marketing piece: a two-page spread in the Portland edition of *Affluent Living* magazine with a "crashing emergency" deadline to meet the requirements for its premiere issue in the local market.

A stationery package, brochure, packaging, collateral items, billboard, signage, a PR packet and other items were developed using that first ad design as inspiration. Color ads for *Portland Monthly* and the regional edition of *Better Homes & Gardens* followed, as did black-and-white and color ads for local newspapers. The award-winning full-page ad was actually rejected by *Vanity Fair* magazine, which requested changes to the design and content if the ad were to be published. Dr. VanderVeer stood true to her brand and refused to alter the successful advertising program piece. The new company look was also used in television commercials and on the center's website.

The almost immediate result of the rebranding efforts was a greater public awareness of Dr. VanderVeer and her business. Many new clients specifically mentioned the new look and said it influenced their decision to become a customer.

⌃ Redesigned billboard

⌃ Redesigned front and back of business card, envelope and letterhead

⌃ Previous billboard prior to name change

⌃ Previous business card prior to name change

شركة لابجيت للتجارة العامة والمقاولات ذ.م.م.
LaBaguette General Trading & Contracting Co. W.L.L.

Eng. Ahmed Al Homoud
Chairman

Ihab A. Bou Hassan
Catering Manager

Tel.: (+965) 533 3311
Fax: (+965) 533 0000
Mob.: (+965) 695 0083
Jabriya - Block 11 - St. 108
P.O. Box 22193 Safat 13082 Kuwait
E-mail: ihab@labaguette.com.kw

شركة لابجيت للتجارة العامة والمقاولات ذ.م.م.
LaBaguette General Trading & Contracting Co. W.L.L.

ص.ب: ٢٢١٩٣ الصفاة الكويت ١٣٠٨٢ – تلفون: ٥٣٢٣٣١١ (٩٦٥) – فاكس: ٥٣٣٠٠٠٠ (٩٦٥)
P.O.Box: 22193 Safat Kuwait 13082 - Tel.: (+965) 5333311 - Fax: (+965) 5330000

ص.ب: ٢٢١٩٣ الصفاة الكويت ١٣٠٨٢ – تلفون: ٥٣٢٣٣١١ (٩٦٥) – فاكس: ٥٣٣٠٠٠٠ (٩٦٥) – رأس المال المدفوع ١,٥٠٠,٠٠٠ د.ك.
P.O.Box: 22193 Safat Kuwait 13082 - Tel.: (+965) 5333311 - Fax: (+965) 5330000 - Paid up capital KD 1,500,000
www.labaguette.com.kw

ص.ب: ٢٢١٩٣ الصفاة
5330311 - Fax: (+965) 5330000

La Baguette

PROJECT:
LaBaguette identity
and brand redesign

DESIGN FIRM:
Paragon Marketing
Communications

LOCATION:
Salmiya, Kuwait

CREATIVE DIRECTOR:
Louai Alasfahani

DESIGNER:
Khalid Al-Rifaie

The La Baguette chain of sixteen outlets was established in Kuwait in 1983. It was the first chain of its kind in Kuwait and was a huge success. As the years went by, many of the founders and/or key members of La Baguette departed to start their own operations, which competed directly with the La Baguette brand. As a result, the brand suffered in both quality and product design, which led to financial loss and the recent sale of the company to a group of entrepreneurs—the client of Paragon Marketing Communications.

The new owners have invested heavily in developing a superior range of improved products intended for the local market. Still, they wanted to maintain the La Baguette name since the La Baguette brand enjoys a high level of brand awareness and recognition despite the negative connotations of the past few years.

The owners agreed upon a solution that was simple in theory—

^ Previous logo

^ Redesigned logo
<<Redesigned stationery package

^ Redesigned product boxes

^ Previous product boxes

^ Redesigned print ad

A symbol of quality   harvested from Nature

^ Redesigned print ad

^ Previous print ad

^ Redesigned storefront treatment

^ Previous storefront treatment

^ Redesigned vehicle signage

^ Previous vehicle signage

"keep the name, change everything else"—in order to communicate the positive change. In reality, this was not an easy task, as Paragon had to develop a totally new and different visual identity. The designers first created a modern logo that clearly differentiates today's La Baguette from the previous logo and those of competitors. The new logo eventually appeared on everything, including the interior design, stationery, external and internal signage, employee uniforms, product packaging, delivery vehicle livery, print media advertisements, new product photography, and promotional materials for events held at various outlets.

By utilizing all of the above tools and methods, Paragon Marketing Communications was able to rejuvenate the La Baguette brand. By elevating its image and updating its look, which directly contributed to increasing the brand's market share in a record time frame, La Baguette regained its position as a market leader. A rejuvenated image can not only keep a client base, but also help attracts new customers.

Giving Form to Electronic Information

Carrie Delente
cdelente@enforme.com

INTERACTIVE

| P | 301/694.0273 |
| F | 301/694.0833 |

www.enforme.com

241 East 4th St.   Suite 205   Frederick, MD 21701

www.enforme.com

241 East 4th St.   Suite 205   Frederick, MD 21701

INTERACTIVE

| P | 301/694.0273 |
| F | 301/694.0833 |

Giving Form to Electronic Information

INTERACTIVE

www.enforme.com

241 East 4th St.   Suite 205   Frederick, MD 21701

www.enforme.com

241 East 4th St.   Suite 205   Frederick, MD 21701

Enforme Interactive

PROJECT:

Enforme Interactive
logo redesign

DESIGN FIRM:

Octavo Designs

LOCATION:

Frederick, Maryland

ART DIRECTOR:

Sue Hough

DESIGNERS:

Mark Burrier, Sue Hough

Enforme Interactive brought in Octavo Designs for a total redesign of their logo. They wanted to move away from the emphasis placed on the *E* of their name to devise a trademark that complimented the new tagline, "Giving Form To Electronic Information."

The designers moved the emphasis to the center of the logo for balance and created a spiral wave shape, which alludes to "giving form." Introduction of the vivid green, a more modern shade, updates the color palette. This redesign became the basis of a complete corporate identity overhaul for the company's print materials and website.

⋀ Redesigned logo

<<Redesigned label, business card, envelope and letterhead

⋀ Previous logo

UNION
LEASING

Corporate Leasing | Government Programs | Rental Car Programs | Remarketing Solutions | Planning Services | Fleet Operations

Union Leasing

PROJECT:
Union Leasing identity

DESIGN FIRM:
Brainforest, Inc.

LOCATION:
Chicago, Illinois

ART DIRECTOR:
Nils Bunde

DESIGNERS:
Drew Larson, Jonathan Amen

Union Leasing began providing vehicles for businesses in 1955. Since then, they've grown into a customer-focused leader in fleet management. They sought a visual identity that not only reflected that change but also set the tone for the future of their company. Brainforest helped them roll out a dynamic new visual presence.

Their existing materials were inconsistent. Two logos existed, one for print and one for web, and there were no clear visual identity guidelines that established font, color and grid usage for collateral systems. Printed materials were sparse and not cohesively planned.

Brainforest began by helping Union Leasing define their brand, working with them to develop a value proposition, mission statement and the "U-First" customer pledge. From that brand personality, a new logo, visual identity, website, printed collateral and signage grew.

The new logo incorporates the *U* and *L* in a single image that indicates movement and strength, brought to life with a vibrant, modern color palette. It is used

^ Redesigned logo
<< Redesigned folder

^ Previous logos

on all UL materials from print to electronic.

Union Leasing's original stationery system contained dozens of components, having been developed piece by piece instead of through a process of needs evaluation. Brainforest helped the company eliminate the use, and thus the cost, of so many unrelated pieces and presented UL with a basic system of letterhead, envelopes and business cards.

Brainforest helped Union Leasing develop a flexible system of sales collateral materials that focused on individual sales sheets housed in a folder. This allowed the sales team to present prospective customers customized marketing packets that were consistent in look and tone regardless of what group of products were being highlighted.

And finally, the redesigned website brought it all together, from brand identity to visual identity, in an engaging, user-friendly design.

∧ Previous home page

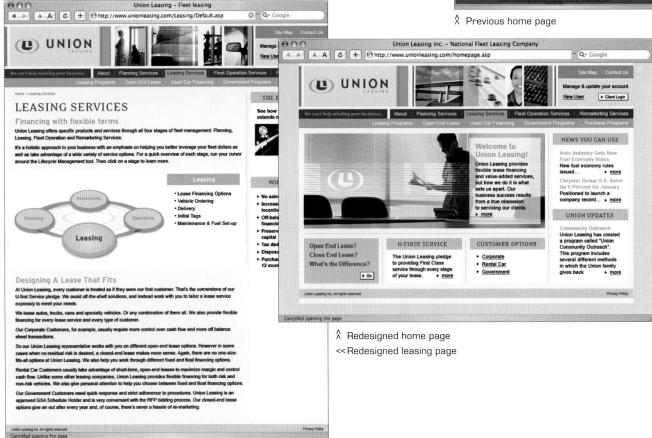

∧ Redesigned home page
<< Redesigned leasing page

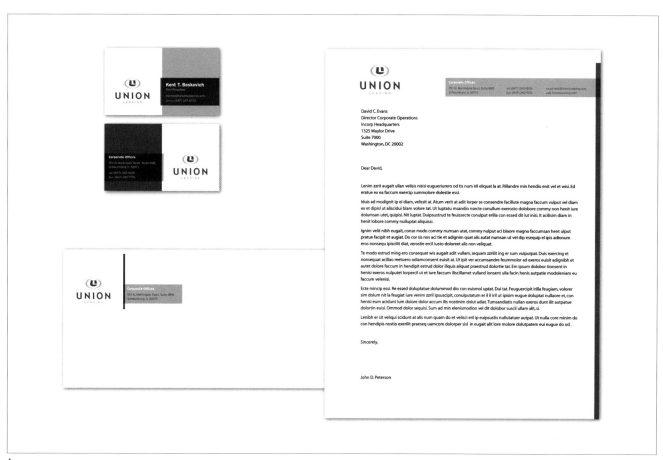

∧ Redesigned stationery

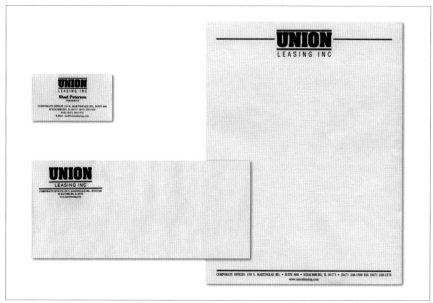

∧ Previous stationery

∧ Redesigned data sheet

glitschka studios

von r. glitschka
illustrative designer

1976 fitzpatrick ave se
salem, or 97306
ph: **971.223.6143**
fx: **503.585.8190**

von@glitschka.com
www.glitschka.com

subscribe to my promo-list
gslist-on@glitschka.com

visit my art blog
www.artbackwash.com

copyright © 2007 glitschka studios

glitschka studios

von r. glitschka
illustrative designer

1976 fitzpatrick ave se
salem, or 97306
ph: **971.223.6143**
fx: **503.585.8190**

von@glitschka.com
www.glitschka.com

Glitschka Studios

PROJECT:
Glitschka Studios identity

DESIGN FIRM:
Glitschka Studios

LOCATION:
Salem, Oregon

ART DIRECTOR/DESIGNER:
Von R. Glitschka

Designers often find it hardest to design for themselves. This proved to be the case for Von Glitschka's redesign of the identity for his own firm. Glitschka started his business in 2002. At the time, he had a lot of local clients and on occasion, worked with larger agencies and firms outside the geographic region. The old identity served its purpose, but over the course of four years, the designer realized the very services he was trying to market were not reflected in his own identity.

"It was a graphic irony," says Glitschka. Glitschka Studios was

∧ Previous logo

∧ Redesigned logo

<< Redesigned letterhead and business cards

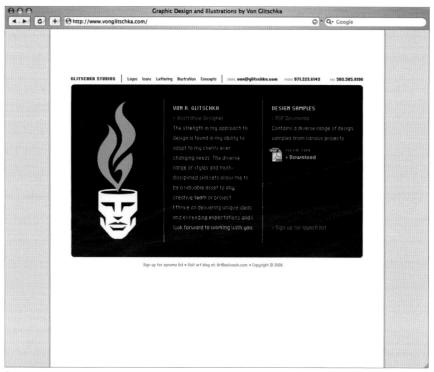

doing more and more agency work as a creative hired gun. Firms sought out the designer because of his unique approach as both a designer and illustrator. They valued Glitschka's ability to work in a variety of styles and liked his unique ideas. The creative ideas he brought to the table helped these agencies present a wider range of possibilities for their clients. He made them look good and was having fun doing it. "My old identity didn't reflect any of this," Glitschka says. "It was cold, impersonal and lacked a creative flair that I was trying to sell." The new mark

⌃ Redesigned website

⌃ Previous business card (front and back)

better represents his abilities, while serving as a practical and immediate sample of Glitschka Studios' work. Glitschka also changed his title to fit this new understanding of the business. He now refers to himself as an illustrative designer. The new mark reflects his strongest asset as a designer, incorporating his illustrative abilities. Notice the integration of the GS letterforms into the flame imagery. Identity crisis resolved.

WORDS OF WISDOM

"If I had to pick one belief that I believe is most detrimental to many designers, it is this: that being a successful designer is all about being a fabulously talented designer. It is not. That is only one part of it. Being a fabulously talented designer is essentially achieving operational excellence, in the same way that Apple makes great iPods or Jimmy Choo makes great shoes. But this 'fabulous talent' does not guarantee that either company is going to be successful or benefit from a return on their design investment. Just because an organization has a fabulous product does not guarantee it will be a success. I think that in order for design to be truly successful, the designer must be able to communicate WHAT it is about a specific design that is remarkable and inspire people to understand it and feel the same way. So, you either have to have an enormous advertising budget—or you need to have strong principles to ignite change."

Debbie Millman
Sterling Brands
New York City, New York
www.debbiemillman.com

organic Arabian Chickpea · Clive's · made with love

Pie. veggie
organic
Arabian Chickpea
An Arabian recipe with chickpeas and tomatoes, the sweetness of apricots and the tang of mint.

organic Aloo Matar Curry · Clive's · made with love

Pie. veggie
organic
Aloo Matar Curry
Fresh potatoes and garden peas in a spicy tomato and coconut sauce with all the enchantment of India.

organic Chestnut Cassoulet · Clive's · made with love

Pie. veggie
organic
Chestnut Cassoulet
Haricot beans, onions, cabbage, tomatoes, chestnuts and herbs - a French delicacy!

organic Creamy Mushroom · Clive's · made with love
Pie. veggie
organic
Creamy Mushroom
Fresh chestnut mushrooms cooked with onions and herbs in a creamy sauce.

organic Greek Lentil & Olive · Clive's · made with love

Pie. veggie
organic
Greek Lentil & Olive
A recipe from sunny Greece with tomatoes, potatoes, brown lentils and kalamata olives.

organic Hungarian Goulash · Clive's · made with love

Pie. veggie
organic
Hungarian Goulash
A vegetarian goulash with fresh vegetables, tasty soya chunks and lots of paprika.

organic Mexican Chilli · Clive's · made with love

Pie. veggie
organic
Mexican Chilli
Tangy tomatoes, fresh vegetables, kidney beans and sweetcorn with all the colour and spice of Mexico.

organic Rosemary & Potato · Clive's · made with love

Pie. veggie
organic
Rosemary & Potato
Delicious potatoes, carrots and onions with tasty vegetarian cheese and a hint of rosemary.

gluten free Aloo Gobi · Clive's · made with love

Pie. organic + veggie
Gluten Free
gluten free
Aloo Gobi
Fresh cauliflower, chunky potatoes and vegetables enriched with Indian spices.
Handmade in Devon.

gluten free French Cassoulet · Clive's · made with love

Pie. organic + veggie
Gluten Free
gluten free
French Cassoulet
Haricot beans, onions, cabbage, tomatoes, chestnuts and herbs - a French delicacy!
Handmade in Devon.

gluten free Cheese & Potato · Clive's · made with love

Pie. organic + veggie
Gluten Free
gluten free
Cheese & Potato
Delicious potatoes, carrots and onions with tasty vegetarian cheese and a hint of rosemary.
Handmade in Devon.

gluten free Lentil & Olive · Clive's · made with love

Pie. organic + veggie
Gluten Free
gluten free
Lentil & Olive
A recipe from sunny Greece with tomatoes, potatoes, brown lentils and kalamata olives.
Handmade in Devon.

gluten free Minty Chickpea · Clive's · made with love

Pie. organic + veggie
Gluten Free
gluten free
Minty Chickpea
An Arabian recipe with chickpeas and tomatoes, the sweetness of apricots and the tang of mint.
Handmade in Devon.

gluten free Vegetable Chilli · Clive's · made with love
Pie. organic + veggie
Gluten Free
gluten free
Vegetable Chilli
Tangy tomatoes, fresh vegetables, kidney beans and sweetcorn with all the colour and spice of Mexico.
Handmade in Devon.

Buckfast Organic Bakery/Clive's

PROJECT:
Clive's rebranding
and repackaging

DESIGN FIRM:
biz-R

LOCATION:
Totnes, Devon, Great Britain

CREATIVE DIRECTOR:
Blair Thomson

DESIGNER:
Tish England

The existing identity and packaging had become dated, inconsistent and uninspiring. It was time to rebrand Buckfast Organic Bakery—"Clive's"—and its range of products. The product line specifically targeted the traditional stereotypical vegetarian market, yet the brand failed to communicate the vibrancy behind the company and its unique selection of vegetarian and gluten-free pies, cakes and pastries.

The objectives of the rebranding were to:

- communicate the dynamic personality of the company
- emphasize the organic nature of the products
- reflect the homemade quality of the products
- convey healthy but fun and tasty recipes
- introduce Clive's to a new generation of health-conscious, brand-aware consumers

The biz-R solution to Clive's identity crisis included a new logo that combines a hand-drawn typeface with clean modern type to communicate the forward-thinking of the company, while conveying the homemade qualities of the products. The tagline "made with love" emphasizes the fact that these

⌃ Redesigned logo
<< Redesigned product packaging

⌃ Previous logo

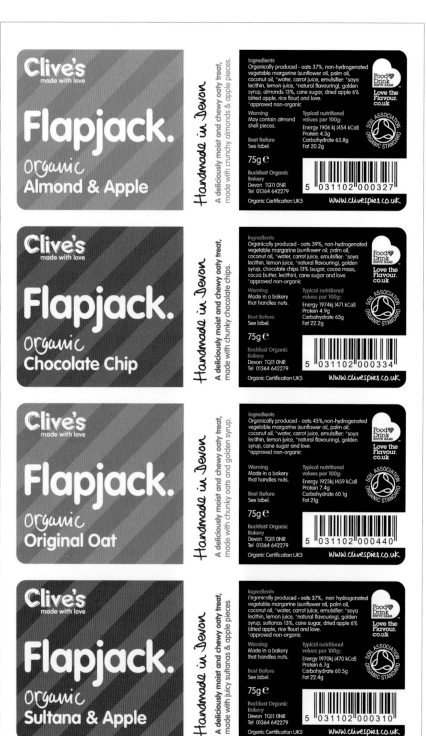

^ Redesigned product packaging

^ Redesigned product packaging

healthy, natural and organic products are handmade.

Handwritten comments and hand-drawn illustrations lend a sense of humor and personality to the brand and give each product a sense of individuality. Distinctive large typography, bright colors and bold photography focusing on the fresh organic ingredients make the brand easily identifiable and make for a contemporary, confident appearance that appeals to a much wider target audience.

The new Clive's identity has been applied across the entire Clive's brand including all packaging, marketing materials, website and vehicles.

∧ Redesigned product packaging

American Design Awards™
REWARDING INNOVATIVE
DESIGN POTENTIAL

American Design Awards™
P O Box 927748
San Diego CA 92192 USA

American Design Awards™
REWARDING INNOVATIVE
DESIGN POTENTIAL

Art Javid
Vice President

Telephone   1 858 777 5522
Email   art.j@americandesignawards.com
Mail   P O Box 927748 San Diego CA 92192
Web   americandesignawards.com

American Design Awards™
REWARDING INNOVATIVE
DESIGN POTENTIAL

Mailing Address
P O Box 927748
San Diego CA 92192 USA

Web / URL
americandesignawards.com

Message Center / Fax
1 858 777 5522

Monthly Design Contest

Winter Semi-Annual

Summer Semi-Annual

American Design Awards

PROJECT:
American Design
Awards identity

DESIGN FIRM:
Graphicwise, Inc.

LOCATION:
Irvine, California

ART DIRECTORS:
Kevin & Art Javid

DESIGNERS:
Kevin & Art Javid

The old American Design Awards identity was dull and unattractive, and its logo and lettering were very similar to some established organizations that shared the same acronym. The challenge was to break out of these dreary boundaries and explore some distinctive colors, fonts and layouts for the new identity, thereby establishing a fresh new beginning for the organization.

Graphicwise owners Kevin and Art Javid, who also cofounded the American Design Awards, agreed to take on the task of restructuring the ailing identity. Being both the client and the designer is always a challenge, but it also allows for flexibility and out-of-the-box creativity. The only restriction: to keep the five round color palettes implemented by the original design team in 2000.

Graphicwise took a fresh approach to the design and rearranged the logo using vibrant colors, distinctive fonts, and classic colors throughout the stationery and website to bring them back to life. Graphicwise also created several unique sub-logos for the monthly and semi-annual design contests, a more visually inviting way for designers to convey information about these.

Since the makeover, the American Design Awards have enjoyed a huge surge in popularity among designers and website visitors.

^ Previous stationery
<< Redesigned stationery

^ Redesigned logo

^ Redesigned event logo

^ Redesigned event logo

^ Redesigned event logo

^ Previous logo

^ Previous event logo

^ Previous event logo

^ Redesigned website

^ Previous website

RIVER LODGE

In 2000 we completed the very special River Lodge, a timberframe structure set just across the back alley from the Inn. Its nine rooms feature luxurious river rock fireplaces, jacuzzi tubs for two, cast iron beds with fine Egyptian cotton linens, televisions, phones, private decks and patios that overlook the glistening river. The best aspects of these rooms are the fantastic views of the famous Lionshead rock, the backside of Vail Mountain, and the Eagle River.

Above: Common Room
River Lodge

Above right: River Rock
Jacuzzi Tub

Right: Missouri Lakes
River Lodge

Originally constructed in 1915 as a residence for
the McBreens, a railroad family, the Minturn Inn
is one of the oldest buildings
we renovated the home into
bedroom bed and breakfast
conveniences. Our distinctiv
feature hand-crafted log bea
down comforters and quilts
antler chandeliers, river ro
many other memorable tou

Minturn Inn
Minturn, Colorado

Minturn Inn

PROJECT:
Minturn Inn logo, stationery
and brochure design

DESIGN FIRM:
b-design

LOCATION:
San Diego, California

CREATIVE DIRECTOR/DESIGNER:
Carey Jones

The previous identity for the Minturn Inn was a basic type treatment of the name in the University Roman font. It was used on signage juxtaposed against the rustic Rocky Mountain lodge, which was housed in a refurbished 1915 Colorado log structure.

The Minturn Inn desired a clean symbol that could be used with or without the type treatment and still brand the business. The image would adorn hats, shirts, mugs and other promotional items. It needed to be simple and clean for embroidery, screenprinting and other applications. The inn is actually a mountain log cabin, with the household furnishings and hand railings of the inn being handcrafted from local aspen trees, so the client wanted the identity to reflect nature and the outdoors.

An aspen leaf symbol, created by b-design, became the focal point for the logo process. After exploration of several options, the clients determined that the leaf's organic imagery produced a strong, easily recognized and memorable symbol that reflects

Minturn Inn

Minturn, Colorado

^ Redesigned logo
<< Redesigned promotional brochure

THE MINTURN INN

A MOUNTAIN BED & BREAKFAST

^ Previous logo

^ Redesigned stationery

the outdoor lifestyle of the clients, the local area and the target market of the inn.

The resulting new look, introduced in signage and printed materials, has helped the owners position the Minturn Inn as one of the premiere bed and breakfasts in the region.

WORDS OF WISDOM

"Look. Learn. Listen.

Look at the visual aspects of the company that are currently being used, and those that have been used in the past. Take a good look at the identity and branding of the client's perceived competition and what you consider to be peers in their industry. When visiting the client's place of business, do a thorough visual inventory of how the existing identity impacts the workplace.

Learn about the history and culture of the business or organization. Develop an understanding of the manner in which the client has done business, marketed their efforts and visually conveyed the business image to their target market over the years. Learn what you can about customer perceptions of the client's efforts—and evaluate if that is what the client thinks they are actually projecting. Confirm the reasons the client feels/thinks a redesign of the corporate identity is required or desired.

Listen to what the client is really saying as the requirements and desires for the new identity are discussed. Understand the sometimes unspoken attachment to the existing identity—from the emotional and historical perspective of the client and their longtime employees and/or customer base. Pay as much attention to what the client dislikes as to what they like."

Jeff Fisher
Jeff Fisher LogoMotives
Portland, Oregon
www.jfisherlogomotives.com

URBANOS

PROJECT:
URBANOS identity

DESIGN FIRM:
MyBrand

LOCATION:
Lisbon, Portugal

ART DIRECTOR:
Rui Roquete

DESIGNER:
A team project

The logistics market is now in a mature stage, and achieving increased revenue is very dependent upon strong communication and a clear and aggressive commercial strategy.

This Portuguese group decided to rebrand its business with the purpose of achieving growth across all the segments it serves through raised customer awareness of its inherent service quality. The solution was in the statement: "URBANOS—We make it possible."

The new brand communicates the idea of deep efficiency and professionalism stemming from the integration of the entire range of services any customer can obtain from the business and its associated group. It has been implemented across all media including vehicle signage, communications materials and online content.

The URBANOS logotype symbolizes a group of elements working strongly together in a visual representation of the integration of services under the URBANOS brand.

The selected blue is representative of calmness and cleanliness.

MyBrand helped the business achieve its goal of raising customer awareness of its full range of logistical services with the identity redesign. The rebranding has led to a rapid rise in cross-sales of URBANOS' services, leading the business to achieve its commercial strategy and raise profit levels.

^ Previous logo

^ Redesigned logo

<< Redesigned T-shirt, structure and vehicle signage

 CAKE BATTER

 SUGAR FREE

 BLACK BERRY

 FOAM

 TRUFFLE

 BANANA

 BROWNIE

 PIE

 PUMPKIN PIE

 DREAMSICLE

 REESE'S PIECES®

 GRAHAM CRACKER

 CONE

 HOT DRINKS

 FAVORITE TOPPING

 WOWIECCINO

 HAZELNUT

 BEVERAGE

 TOFFEE

 COOKIE DOUGH

 BUNDT CAKE

 CONCRETE

 M&M'S®

 CHOCOLATE

 REESE'S®

 COTTON CANDY

 LATTÉ

 LEMON

 APPLE PIE

 IRISH CREME

 ALMOND

 PINEAPPLE

 HOT DOG

 ON ICE

 RICE KRISPIES®

 OREO®

 WHIPPED CREAM

 CARAMEL

 PRETZEL

 CHERRY

 MILK

 MINT

 PEANUT BUTTER

 MARSH MALLOW

 ESPRESSO

 PEACH

 MANGO

 NERDS®

 NEW YORK CHEESECAKE

 CHOCOLATE CHIP

 GUMMY WORMS

 WILD CHERRY

 BLUEBERRY

 COCONUT FLAKES

 VANILLA

 HALF & HALF

 DECAF

 VANILLA CUSTARD

 CINNAMON SUGAR

 RAINBOW SPRINKLES

 LIME

 CHOCOLATE SPRINKLES

 MANDARIN ORANGE

 PECAN

 BUTTER FINGER®

 SHORTCAKE

 MALT BALL

 SNICKERS®

 HOT FUDGE

 BUTTER SCOTCH

 STRAWBERRY

 SMOOOTHIE

 RASPBERRY

 ESPRESSO SHOT

 WHITE CHOCOLATE

 CHOCOLATE CUSTARD

 HEATH®

 SUNDAE

 CUP

 ANDE'S® MINT

 COFFEE

Sheridan's Lattés and Frozen Custard

PROJECT:
Sheridan's Lattés and Frozen Custard identity and rebranding

DESIGN FIRM:
Willoughby Design Group

LOCATION:
Kansas City, Missouri

CREATIVE/ART DIRECTORS:
Ann Willoughby, Megan Semrick, Zack Shubkagel

DESIGNERS:
Nate Hardin, Jessica McEntire

Sheridan's Lattés and Frozen Custard is an established local franchise with thirty locations in twelve states. It introduced frozen custard to several markets, including Kansas City. After seven successful years, Sheridan's realized the need to update its identity in order to compete more effectively. They also need-ed help integrating a line of latté drinks to their product mix.

The Willoughby Design Group design process began with an analysis of the existing Sheridan's logo. The firm discovered there was great equity in the Sheridan's name but not as much with Wowie, the mascot. The client was communicating a lot of messages,

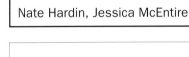

^ Previous logo

^ Redesigned logo and logotypes

^ Redesigned logo
<< Redesigned company "DNA"

including the tagline, "Made Fresh All Day." The design process next focused on the Sheridan's type treatment, without Wowie.

Willoughby presented Sheridan's with three focused directions for their identity redesign. The process involved numerous sketches and drafts. A team of three designers was asked to focus their design on either Simple Comforts; Fresh Delicious Treats; or Fun, Hip Experience. This variety allowed a range of comfort for the client and the opportunity to reposition the identity. Close attention was given to making each palette different while maintaining something to evoke taste. In order to give the client a big-picture look at each of the directions, a template was developed that extended the identity beyond the logo to building, signage, ads, packaging and vehicles. This also became the framework for the design firm's extension of the approved direction.

One of the biggest challenges the design team faced was to redesign and reposition Wowie, the sacred cow mascot. To incorporate this beloved part of the client's original identity, Willoughby had to morph the bovine into a hipper animal. It was requisite to maintain his bullhood and coolness. However, the design team felt the original cowbell and hay bale worked against this image. Some complained his snout was that of a pig. There was much to improve.

One of the most important facets of the new identity is an entirely new system of icons called Treat DNA™. Willoughby designed over seventy-five icons to catalog Sheridan's extensive list of toppings, ingredients and options. Using iconography that ranges from literal (a banana for banana) to the more esoteric (George Washington for cherries), the icons are designed to capture attention, make people do some deciphering and point out the range of possibilities. While originally intended to help navigate

^ Redesigned storefront

^ Previous storefront

^ Redesigned walk-up menu

^ Redesigned posters

^ Previous menu boards

⋀ Redesigned banners

⋀ Redesigned menu cover

⋀ Redesigned catering brochure cover

⋀ Redesigned cup sleeve

⋀ Previous product design

the menu, the icons became overwhelming. So now Treat DNA is implemented in the client's advertising, promotions and as a decorative motif used in environmental graphics and packaging.

While Sheridan's worked on developing and perfecting the latté side of the business, Willoughby developed a voice and look specific to the new business. Hoping to attract new consumers, the communication is more sophisticated and targeted at an adult audience without being too pretentious. The latté look comprises steamy patterns for hot drinks, frosty textures for the iced lattés and a warm palette.

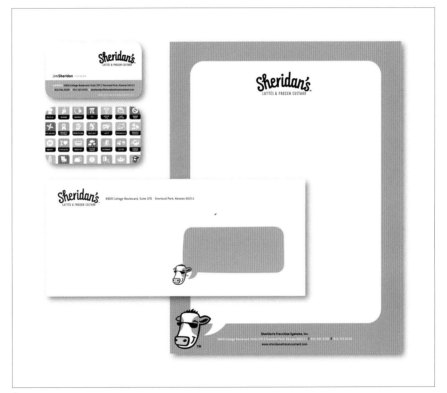

15407 Main Street #104 | Mill Creek, WA 98012
Tel: 425-337-1338 | Fax: 425-337-1663

RoyalReinsch   5407 Main Street #104
Mill Creek, WA 98012
Tel: 425-337-1338
Fax: 425-337-1663
www.belleprov.com

belle provence
FINE LIVING... | SPIRITED GIFTS | SINCE 1983

15407 Main Street #104 | Mill Creek, WA 98012
Tel: 425-337-1338 | Fax: 425-337-1663

Belle Provence

PROJECT:
Belle Provence
identity redesign

DESIGN FIRM:
John Silver Design

LOCATION:
Bothell, Washington

CREATIVE DIRECTOR/DESIGNER:
John Silver

Belle Provence started as a boutique-style shop in a quaint shopping area with a crafty, country theme. After twenty-two years of success in the little village mall, it was time to upgrade the retail products and move to a higher-end location. The upscale town of Mill Creek, Washington, had just opened a new shopping center and Belle Provence, with its new products in tow, settled in. John Silver Design was approached with a request to bring the store's twenty-two-year-old identity up to par with the shop's new surroundings. The pomegranate flourish that separates Belle from Provence solidifies an organic sense in order that appeals to an already solid client base who would follow the store from the Country Village shopping center to the chic boutique in Mill Creek. The black and white palette selected for the logo itself is extremely versatile and adds a touch of class to the wide variety of products and colors inside the shop.

The client, owner Diane Reinscha, was very open to new ideas and brought a great deal of creativity to the table herself. Over the course of the design process, she had chosen several textile patterns and color schemes. The designer and client settled on

^ Redesigned logo
<< Redesigned stationery

^ Previous logo

^ Redesigned postcard

^ Redesigned storefront signage

^ Redesigned storefront signage

a black and lime green palette for stationery, labels and indoor signage. The palette reflects the modern, international feel of the products within the store in a subtle way. The new identity has been received exceedingly well by Belle Provence clientele, faithful and new alike.

WORDS OF WISDOM

"First, clearly define your company's expectations of the identity redesign—why are you doing this, what are you hoping to gain as a result and what extent of change are you willing to consider? Then revisit your current brand positioning and ask if it is still relevant. Don't hire a firm and kick off the project until you have completed these internal exercises. If senior leadership isn't aligned on these issues, it can get costly and frustrating for everyone involved.

Provide your design firm with as much information as you can about your company, competition and target audiences. Then allow the designers to interview internal stakeholders and customers firsthand—there is no better way for them to understand your business and discover the insights that will drive creative thinking.

If your design firm starts discussing design solutions before discussing the goals and criteria of the project and your business, fire them immediately and start over with a new firm.

Be prepared for new ideas and to embrace change.

Don't let a designer or design firm do something just because they think it looks cool. Make them justify their work with how it supports your business and your brand."

Bob Domenz
Avenue Marketing & Communications
Chicago, Illinois
www.avenue-inc.com

Vickie Lea Designs, Inc.
custom landscaping & design

P.O. Box 540376
Omaha, 68154

402.707.2020 [cell]
402.496.2051 [off.]

Vickie Lea Designs, Inc.
custom landscaping & design

Vickie Lea Coonrod
owner/designer

P.O. Box 540376
Omaha, NE 68154

402.707.2020 [cell]
402.496.2051 [off.]
www.vickieleadesigns.com

Vickie Lea Designs

PROJECT:
Vickie Lea Designs, Inc., identity

DESIGN FIRM:
RDQ (Rdqlus Design Quantum)

LOCATION:
Omaha, Nebraska

ART DIRECTOR/DESIGNER:
Steve Gordon, Jr.

Vickie Lea Designs is an up-and-coming lawn and landscape design company that offers more customized landscaping solutions than competitors. Service from VLD is top-notch, however, the company's identity wasn't on par with larger, more established companies in the area. Its original identity lacked any true mark that could serve as a strong logo, and there was no clear organization of information. In short, there was no identity to begin with. VLD's ability to compete in the market was hampered from a recognition standpoint. Having a well-designed identity would give the look and feel of an established, well-run and capable business.

The solution was a strong iconic logo and bold colors, with business cards and vehicle signage playing off of the growing fame of VLD's bright yellow trucks. Customer response to the more polished company's image was overwhelmingly positive, and VLD's collaborative use of the identity materials resulted in higher visibility in the market.

^ Redesigned vehicle signage

^ Redesigned logo

<<Redesigned letterhead (front and back) and business card (front and back)

^ Previous logos

RUBY
receptionists

December 6, 2005

John Donaldson
Donaldson Law Firm
4478 Maple Ave
Milton, NY 10045

Dear John,

On behalf of the Ruby team, I would like to thank
choosing Ruby as your virtual receptionist. By no
account has been activated and hopefully, you a
your new service.

Enclosed is detailed information on your spec
for your reference. If you have any questions,
hesitate to contact us.

Sincerely,

Jill Nelson
President

P.S. There's no better compliment tha
referral from a client! Refer an associ
credit on your next bill (certain restri

866-611-RUBY   RUBY R

Your
GUIDE
to Ruby Receptionists

Ruby Receptionists

PROJECT:
Ruby Receptionists
identity rebrand

DESIGN FIRM:
Sockeye Creative

LOCATION:
Portland, Oregon

CREATIVE DIRECTOR:
Peter Metz

ILLUSTRATOR:
Nila Aye

COPYWRITER:
Norm Sajove

DESIGNERS:
Erica Brinker, Peter Metz,
Robert Wees

WorkSource, Inc., came to Sockeye Creative in January 2005 with a simple request: design a new logo. The company had streamlined their basic business model. They wanted a fresh look, one that better communicated their new focus—a virtual receptionist service.

The company's target market was small- to mid-size businesses that didn't want (or couldn't afford) a full-time receptionist, yet wanted to provide personal phone service for customers. From a remote location, WorkSource would answer the phone with a custom greeting. They'd screen,

∧ Previous logo before name change

∧ Redesigned logo with name change
<< Redesigned customer kit

announce and transfer calls any-where. They'd take messages, offer voicemail and even answer questions. They'd be professional, dependable and friendly. Basically, they'd offer all the benefits of having a personal on-site receptionist at a fraction of the cost. It was a catchy idea, and by the time Sockeye Creative came onboard, WorkSource had already acquired a handful of customers across the country.

Sockeye Creative's first thought? WorkSource needed more than just a new logo. They needed a whole new name. Work-Source, Inc., just didn't reflect their fun, personable approach to doing business. It wasn't memorable, and it didn't say anything about the incredible service they provided. The design team told the client that renaming the company should be part of the rebrand. They agreed.

Almost immediately, the design firm envisioned something with a look and feel that would evoke the 1940s and 1950s—classic eras when providing excellent customer service was paramount. Back then, you'd drive into a gas station and the attendant would sprint to your car. He'd check your tires, wash your windows and fill your tank. He'd do it all with a smile.

∧ Redesigned letterhead

At some point, Sockeye decided that using a woman's name from that era—one that sounded as if it belonged to a secretary or front-desk receptionist—would be the way to go. A list of hundreds of names was compiled, culled primarily from census records, old yearbooks and the family trees of Sockeye employees. After three weeks, there was a winner. WorkSource, Inc., became Ruby Receptionists.

Once a name was established, the focus shifted to creating an identity. Again, the search was for something that was fun and personable, even playful. Sockeye's creative team developed custom, hand-drawn letterforms for the Ruby logo. A unique color palette of magenta, grapefruit and orange was selected. Sockeye Creative hired freelance artist Nila Aye was hired to create whimsical illustrations that were simple yet

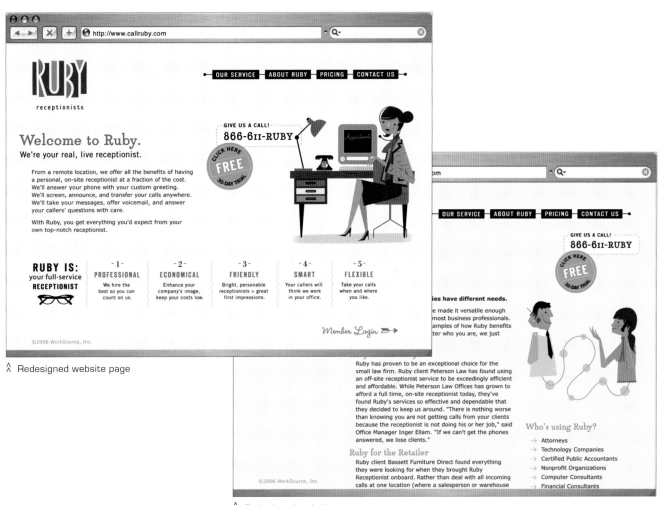

^ Redesigned website page

^ Redesigned website page

expressive and perfectly captured the personality of Ruby. Everything was rolled into new materials and a new website.

Today, Ruby's business is skyrocketing. The company increased its customer base from fifty to just over five thousand in less than two years. "Switching to Ruby literally doubled the number of new clients we get each month," gushes Jill Nelson, president and cofounder. When the rebrand rolled out with CallRuby.com in April 2005, the average number of new clients per month jumped from twelve to twenty-six. "In the beginning, we had three receptionists. Now, twenty-five charismatic professionals answer phone calls nearly 24 hours a day, seven days a week."

The effect rebranding has had on their corporate culture is equally as impressive. Hiring new employees is easier and keeping them is not a problem. Internal promotions are more fun and exciting. Around the office, receptionists even refer to each other as "Rubies."

Every day, all across America, more and more attorneys, retailers, consultants, stockbrokers, service professionals, and sales reps discover Ruby for the first time—and wonder how they ever did business without them.

All it took was a new name and a new identity.

Los Angeles
Mission
The Crossroads of Hope

Brenda D. Springer
Development Officer

Telephone / Fax
(714) 953-3241 / (714) 541-0600

Corporate Office
2333 N. Broadway, Suite 130
Santa Ana, California 92706

Mission Location
303 East 5th Street
Los Angeles, California 90013

Email / Website
BSpringer@lamission.net
losangelesmission.org

Los Angeles
Mission
The Crossroads of Hope

Los Angeles
Mission
The Crossroads of Hope

P.O. Box 55900
Los Angeles, CA 90055-0630

Mailing Address:
P.O. Box 55900
Los Angeles, CA 90055-0630

Telephone:
(213) 629-1227
(213) 629-0036 *fax*

Web:
losangelesmission.org

CLIENT IN CRISIS

Los Angeles Mission

PROJECT:
Los Angeles Mission identity redesign

DESIGN FIRM:
Graphicwise, Inc.

LOCATION:
Irvine, California

ART DIRECTORS/DESIGNERS:
Kevin & Art Javid

The Los Angeles Mission provides hope and opportunity to the homeless and underprivileged. Their corporate identity was outdated, mismatched and lacked the energy the client was after. According to the client, the main goal was to communicate hope and new beginnings to those seeking help, while keeping their motto, "The Crossroads of Hope" intact.

Furthermore, although the Los Angeles Mission is a Christian organization, it felt that the dominant cross within the old logo may have been discouraging to non Christians in need of help, so Graphicwise, Inc., was asked to come up with some sort of a solution.

The team at Graphicwise considered icons that would convey hope and new beginnings while staying within the client's requests. After weeks of tinkering with various icons, Graphicwise came up with the idea of a rising sun and a lit pathway to symbolize new beginnings. The only challenge left was to incorporate a cross into the logo. After seeing the Los Angeles Mission's motto, it became clear where the cross could be placed without being too overwhelming—right in the center of the logo as the crossroad.

^ Redesigned identity
<<Redesigned stationery package

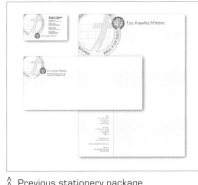

^ Previous stationery package

^ Previous logo

SUMMER 2005

IN
TOUCH

SCANSOFT puts PDF
power in your price range

Explore the creative genius
of ADOBE Creative Suite

Dishing on MICROSOFT'S
SQL Server 2005

First glimpse: MICROSOFT
Visual Studio 2005

Rest assured with
WEBSENSE Web
Security Suite

Microsoft recognizes
Software Spectrum

THE ULTIMATE RESOURCE FOR EFFECTIVE
PLANNING
MICROSOFT ENTERPRISE PROJECT MANAGEMENT

Software Spectrum

PROJECT:

InTouch newsletter

DESIGN FIRM:

MasonBaronet

LOCATION:

Dallas, Texas

ART DIRECTOR/DESIGNER:

Willie Baronet

Software Spectrum works with companies to select, purchase and manage software on an enterprise level—thereby helping them control their IT spend. To generate new leads and new revenue sources, they called on MasonBaronet.

What began as a traditional newsletter project quickly evolved into a comprehensive relationship management program—including a printed newsletter, HTML e-mails and web portal. Design elements MasonBaronet incorporated included a new masthead, figurative/consumer-oriented photography, active and engaging headlines and a call-to-action to the web portal for more information.

^ Previous newsletter cover
<< Redesigned newsletter cover

△ Redesigned newsletter interior

△ Redesigned newsletter cover

△ Previous newsletter interiors

^ Redesigned newsletter interior

^ Previous newsletter cover

WORDS OF WISDOM

"The client knows his or her business (or organization) best, and sharing that knowledge with the design firm is critical. The best role any client can play is to share all pertinent information about the business or organization, as well as market research about the brand and target audience, to allow the designer or design firm to be part of the project from the ground floor and up, beginning with setting strategy. Though the client knows his or her brand best; the designer knows design best; therefore, once a reputable design firm is on board, the client should very seriously consider the designer's best solutions."

Robin Landa, Branding and Creative Strategist
New York City, New York
www.robinlanda.com

marketing on the internet

Ecos Consulting

PROJECT:

Ecos Consulting brand identity and new business pitch packet design

DESIGN FIRM:

FullblastInc.com

LOCATION:

Portland, Oregon

CREATIVE DIRECTOR/DESIGNER:

N. Todd Skiles

Ecos Consulting is an environmental consulting company championing energy efficiency in businesses and in the home. The firm is hired by utilities (gas, water and electric) to create campaigns for education/energy efficiency. Its staff has grown recently from eight people to over forty-five people doing business in three states. Local projects became national campaigns. Ecos Consulting was also looking to expand into additional markets such as appliances and the hybrid or biodiesel auto industry.

The business had outgrown its existing identity, and its existing pitch packet did not meet sales needs. The materials used were made primarily of plastic, sending the wrong idea to environmentally conscious prospective clients. The featured item was a three-ring binder filled with more than twenty pages of product sample sheets. The binder overshadowed the more important part of the packet: an off-the-shelf folder holding the proposal and Ecos' qualifications. The shell required an additional envelope for shipping and was susceptible to damage in shipping. The cost of the piece was $5 each in materials and $47 each in employee time to assemble.

FullblastInc.com was hired to design the company's new identity and business pitch packet. A more streamlined pitch packet, with a high impact cover boasting a clean design and unique binding was produced. The back cover features a die cut of the logo and a window highlighting the samples held inside. The packet fits into an off-the-shelf envelope and

∧ Previous presentation package

∧ Redesigned logo
<< Redesigned presentation package

∧ Previous logo

requires less postage. The new packet cost is $12 each—printed, die-cut, bound and assembled—with no expensive employee assembly time.

As a result of the new materials, Ecos Consulting now has a much higher rate of success with its pitches and has grown dramatically in desired markets.

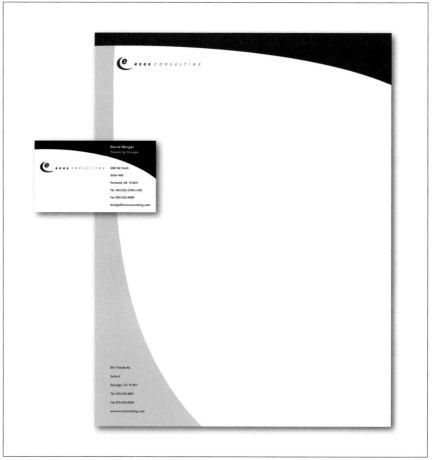

ᗐ Redesigned business card and letterhead

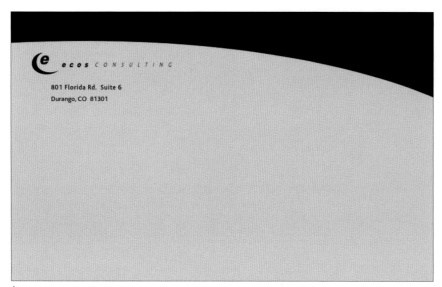

ᗐ Redesigned mailing label

ᗐ Previous business card

^ Redesigned envelope

^ Previous envelope

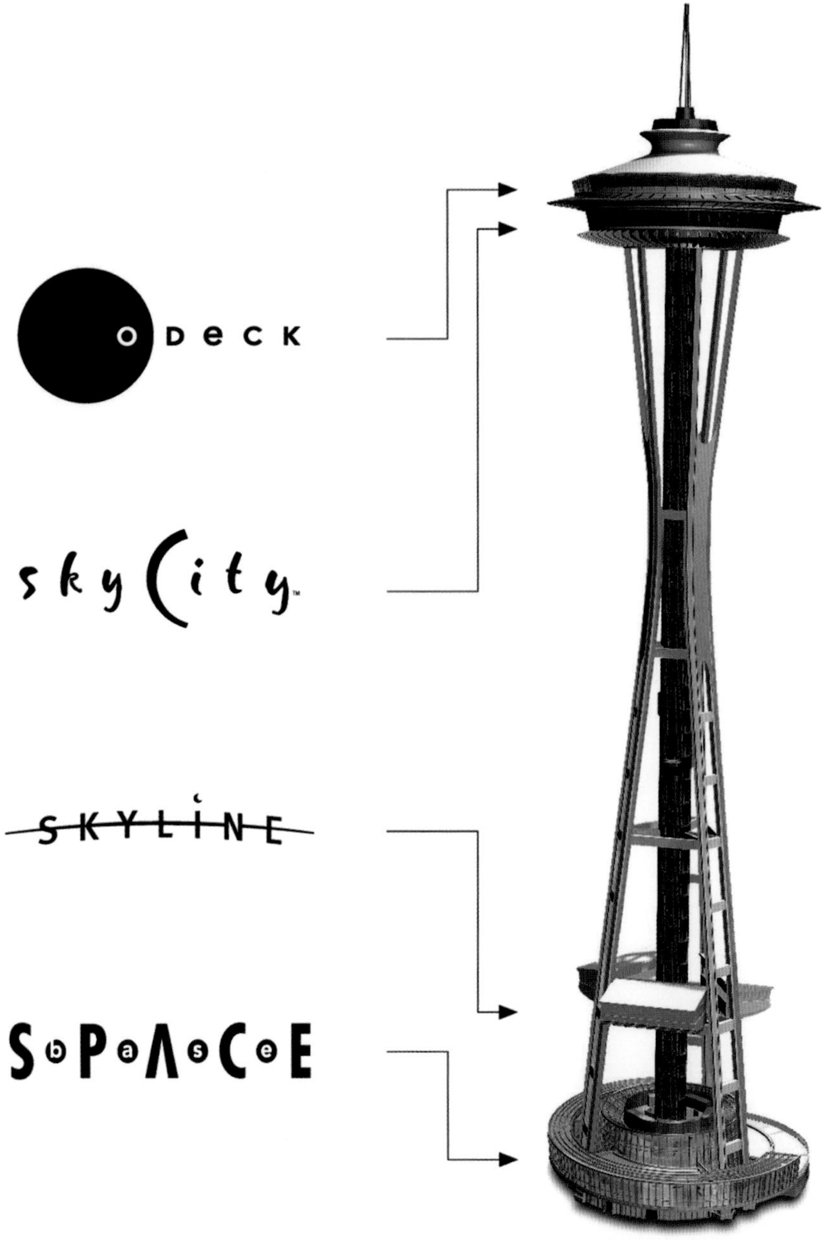

O **DECK**

sky (ity.

~~SKYLINE~~

S•b•P•a•A•s•C•e•E

CLIENT IN CRISIS

Space Needle

PROJECT:
Space Needle identity program

DESIGN FIRM:
Hornall Anderson Design

LOCATION:
Seattle, Washington

DESIGNERS:
Jack Anderson, Mary Hermes,
Gretchen Cook, Julie Lock,
Holly Craven, Elmer dela Cruz,
Belinda Bowling, Andrew Smith,
Alan Florsheim, Cliff Chung

WEB SITE:
Rick Miller, Taka Suzuki,
Roel Nava, Margaret Long,
Alan Draper, Hillary Radbill,
Don Kenoyer

The Space Needle, a world-renowned Seattle icon and city tourist point-of-interest attraction/destination, approached Hornall Anderson Design Works to create a new brand. The idea was to leverage the twenty-first century while retaining a look reminiscent of the original 1962 World's Fair structure. In addition to revamping the corporate logo, the creative team partnered with Tyler Cartier, a naming and branding consultant, to devise several sub-brands to represent the various levels of the Space Needle.

It was imperative for the new identity to serve as a visual interpretation, both respecting the historical value of the Space Needle and communicating its position as a world-class attraction for the

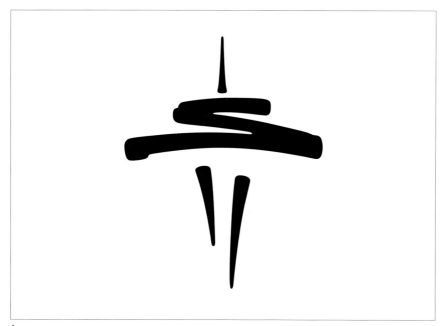

^ Redesigned logo
<<Diagram exhibiting redesigned logos by level

Mary Bacarella
Communications Manager

Space Needle Corporation
203 6th Avenue North
Seattle, WA 98109-5005
Main: (206) 443-9700
Direct: (206) 443-2161, ext.1434
Fax: (206) 441-7415
E-mail: maryba@spaceneedle.com

^ Previous logo on business card

^ Redesigned notebook

^ Redesigned promotional yo-yos

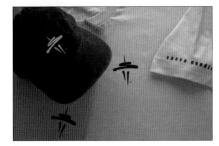

^ Redesigned wearables

^ Redesigned glassware

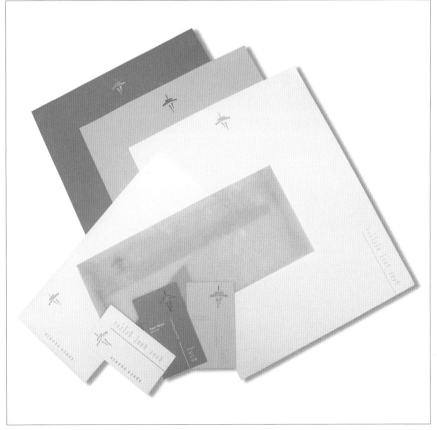

^ Redesigned stationery package

present and the future. Included in the redesign is the creation of a master brand and a series of four closely related brands consisting of SpaceBase—the gift shop at the base of the structure, SkyLine—the 100th level used for events, SkyCity—the 360° rotating restaurant, and O-Deck—the observation deck at the top of the structure. Working together, these brands embody a "vertical village," tying the entire structure into one prominent and memorable brand. As a result, "Live the View" has become the corporate catchphrase, representing the goal of visitors having different experiences at each of the structure's levels.

The comprehensive branding program literally reinvented the way visitors and tourists move through the Space Needle. The architectural firm Callison was enlisted to transform the flow of the entire structure and the visiting experience, including the manner in which people navigate through the Needle. Graphics adorning the upper-level walls highlight city and historical facts, which appeal to both adults and children alike.

Additional structural elements located at the Space Needle's base, coupled with the updated renovations, appeals to locals

^ Redesigned admission tickets

^ Previous collateral

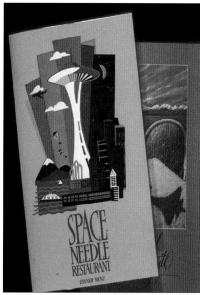

^ Previous menus

and tourists. It's become a point-of-interest destination and is seeing a lot more visitors than in recent years.

In addition to a new identity, Hornall Anderson also created

a comprehensive branding program that included corporate letterhead and business papers, promotional merchandise applications, restaurant collateral and menus, and signage located throughout the structure—both internal and external.

In designing the Space Needle's website, Hornall Anderson communicated the "virtual village" idea—letting visitors "Live the View" by including the sights and activities at each level—rather than just showing landscape views. The designer also implemented web cams. The web cam includes landmark views that promote additional Seattle sites and encourage tourism. By doing this, the site generates revenue through sponsorship from the other sites.

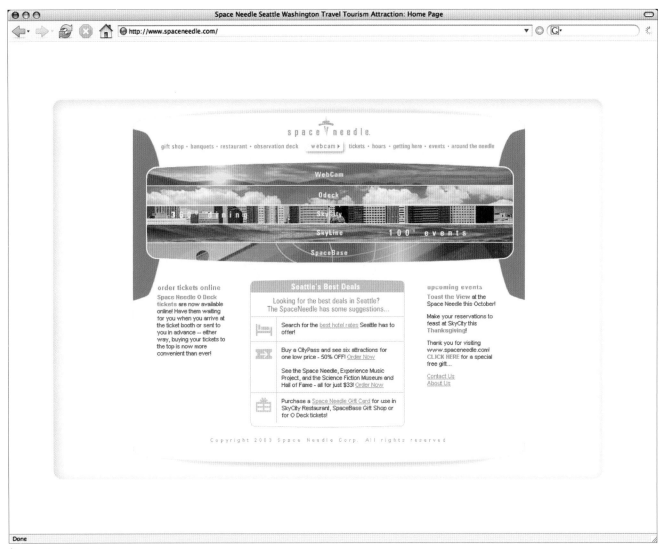

ᚼ Redesigned website

∧ Redesigned banner

∧ Redesigned directional kiosk

∧ Redesigned SpaceBase signage

∧ Redesigned SkyCity restaurant signage

Oregon Department of Forestry

PROJECT:

Oregon Department of Forestry identity redesign

DESIGN FIRM:

Jeff Fisher LogoMotives

LOCATION:

Portland, Oregon

CREATIVE DIRECTOR/DESIGNER:

Jeff Fisher

In its seventy-nine-year history, the Oregon Department of Forestry has been represented by a series of identities. Most recently, in 1971, the department adopted a half-tree logo.

They had been using this logo for nearly two decades when a change was proposed. Many within (and out of) the State of Oregon government agency disliked the image and found that it was confusing to many others. Some thought the thin half-tree graphic conveyed a message of unhealthy forests.

The new logo conveys a much more simplified and organic image, while maintaining some of the inherent formality of a government agency identity. It projected the Department of Forestry's growing involvement and interest in all forest resources, including air, soil, water and trees. The new image is more in line with the Oregon Board of Forestry's new guiding policy document, the Forestry Program for Oregon.

The logo is the department identifier on all printed collateral, vehicles, uniform shoulder patches, the website and other materials. It is widely recognized due to the carving of the logo on signage at the Oregon Department of Forestry headquarters and throughout the state at ranger stations and state forest boundaries.

^ Redesigned logo

<<Redesigned logo on a vehicle and on signage

^ Previous logos

PROJECT:
CHUMS brand identity

DESIGN FIRM:
FullblastInc.com

LOCATION:
Portland, Oregon

CREATIVE DIRECTOR/DESIGNER:
N. Todd Skiles

CLIENT IN CRISIS

CHUMS

Although CHUMS, a manufacturer of eyewear retainers, was one of the first to market with one of the best products in the industry, its sales lagged behind those of its competitors. Six design firms had tackled the challenges of the company's identity over the course of the previous two years, and the brand suffered as a result. Since CHUMS had most recently worked with larger studios, FullblastInc.com embraced this opportunity to deliver big-studio quality work with the attention, flexibility and price that a smaller studio can often provide.

CHUMS carries 32 products in 26 different colors for a confusing 832 variations. Many products, promotional items and hangtags

looked similar, with the same muted colors throughout the product line marketing efforts. With

^ Redesigned T-shirt graphic

^ Redesigned logo
<< Redesigned website pages

^ Previous logo

^ Redesigned T-shirt graphic

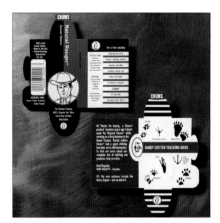

FullblastInc.com's input, CHUMS opted to create a new personality or mini-identity for each product, to define products relative to their function and rename products where necessary, to develop a strong mailing system and to create a high-impact mailer to organize product information.

FullblastInc.com retained the existing logo but altered the usage and colors of the identity. Usage guidelines developed for the client provide direction in all applications and maintain consistency in packaging and promotion efforts. A new color palette of six strong, bright, saturated colors was introduced, along with custom illustrations and photography, and four distinctive die-cut shapes for product presentation.

A custom "Handy User's Guide" connecting the intended use of the product with the activity of the consumer, was also produced. For example, the Waterproof Chum

⌃ Redesigned hangtag

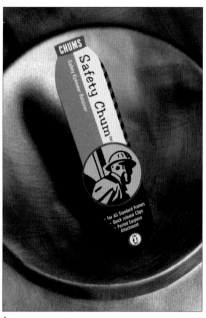

⌃ Redesigned hangtag

⌃ Previous hangtags

included a knot-tying guide; the Safety Chum presented a definition of the haz-mat symbols. An element of humor was also added to the Handy User's Guide. The

Kid's Ranger Chum included camping tips and footprints of a bear, a lion, a deer and an alien, while the Cell Phone Holder Chum listed two hundred country codes and

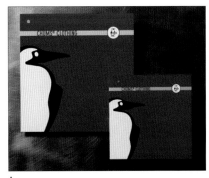

^ Redesigned clothing tags

^ Redesigned product pouch front

^ Redesigned product pouch back

the number for the British Secret Service—followed by the directive "Ask for Bond, James Bond."

An oversized graphic envelope was created to ship a die-cut mailer holding one to six product items and sale sheets. Each product was assigned a color for promotions, allowing for instant identification of the product with or without its hangtag—e.g. if it was red, it was the Chumbo.

The new brand premiered at an industry trade show with six-foot blowups of the hangtag characters next to newly designed displays filled with the same product. Teaser cards mailed out one week earlier set the stage. Catalogs, advertising elements and product

samples filled enthusiastic retailers' bags during the show. A jump in sales greeted the CHUMS sales team upon their return.

FullblastInc.com continued work on the retainer line (including advertising campaigns and an e-commerce website) while diving into the rebrand of the CHUMS clothing line. In fact, FullblastInc.com remained CHUMS' agency of record for the next eighteen months (nine times longer than any agency/studio before or since).

Armed with a cohesive brand, CHUMS enjoyed increased sales, saturation in the U.S. market and expansion into Japan and other previously untouched markets.

^ Redesigned product display card

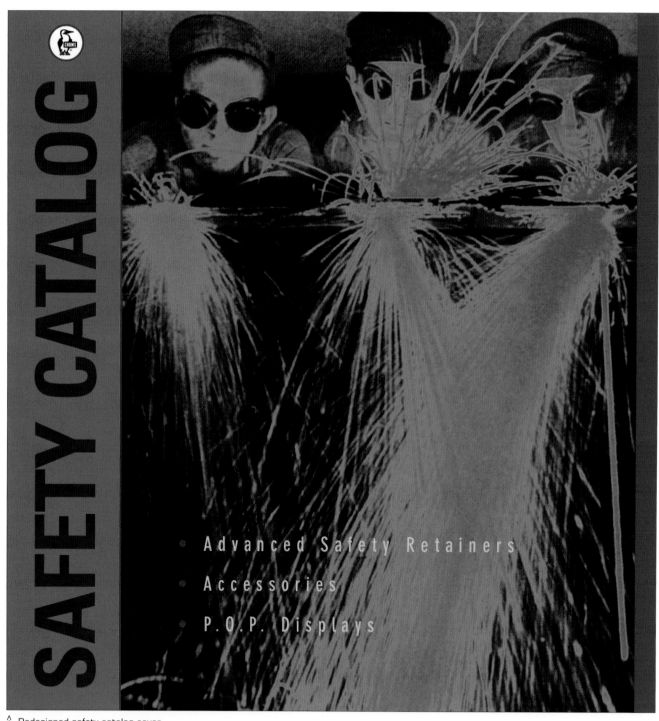

SAFETY CATALOG

- Advanced Safety Retainers
- Accessories
- P.O.P. Displays

∧ Redesigned safety catalog cover

^ Redesigned product catalog

"Best Steaks in the Bay"

STEAKHOUSE & WINERY

Wine Menu

PROJECT:

Pier 39 identity makeover

DESIGN FIRM:

Graphicwise, Inc.

LOCATION:

Irvine, California

ART DIRECTORS/DESIGNERS:

Kevin & Art Javid

CLIENT IN CRISIS

Pier 39 Steakhouse and Winery

Pier 39 Steakhouse and Winery was seeking a fresh new image to revitalize their aging establishment and attract a more diverse clientele. The client complained that the old logo, coloring and atmosphere attracted only long-time locals and "old fishermen-type" individuals, instead of tourists and younger business people looking for a hip upscale restaurant.

Graphicwise, Inc., was asked to create a brand-new identity without any client input or restrictions. The challenge was to make the restaurant stand out amongst dozens of cutting-edge eateries in the area while communicating a rich and elegant vibe.

After experimenting with a wide range of shapes and icons, Graphicwise owners Kevin and Art Javid

^ Previous menu

^ Redesigned logo

<< Redesigned menu

^ Previous logo

^ Redesigned stationery

decided to fiddle around with the idea of a bull as the dominant feature in the logo, after finishing up a delicious steak dinner courtesy of the client. And it worked. They quickly played off San Francisco's colors of gold and burgundy, then implemented an old-style font.

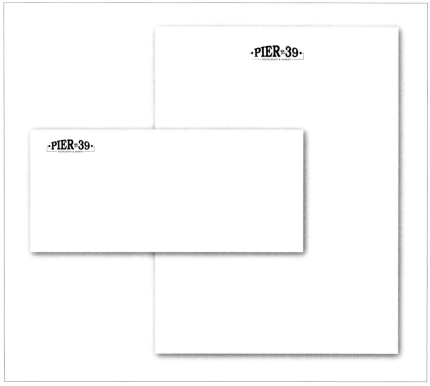

∧ Previous stationery

WORDS OF WISDOM

"No matter what level you begin at, ask the important questions. Who are we? Where are we going? What is our purpose and our underlying mission? How must we behave to achieve them? How are we best understood when we define our parts? Keep asking until you reach the level of leadership that owns the answers."

Tony Spaeth
Identityworks
Rye, New York
www.identityworks.com

VISIT US

Freshman Preview Day
October 29, 2005
Look at life as a Portland State
University student.

Campus Visit Program
Any day, Monday–Friday
Tour campus with a current student,
meet some of our faculty, see on-campus
housing options.

PSU Friday
*February 10, March 10, April 14
and May 12, 2006*
A series of informational sessions and activities.

Transfer Preview
January 13 and April 10, 2006
For community college students considering
a transfer to Portland State University.

PORTLAND STATE UNIVERSITY   **WWW.PDX.EDU/ADMISSIONS**
PORTLAND STATE IS AN AFFIRMATIVE ACTION / EQUAL OPPORTUNITY INSTITUTION

A LEADER IN CHOICE	#1 CYCLING CITY IN AMERICA	STUDENT TO FACULTY RATIO	FOREST PARK	CONNECTED	BURNSIDE SKATE PARK	VIKING FEVER	"AMERICA'S 10 BEST PLACES TO LIVE AND WORK FOR THOSE UNDER 40."	FACTS
Portland State offers more than 120 academic majors, minors and concentrations.	Voted by *Bicycling* magazine, two years in a row.	18:1 AVERAGE CLASS SIZE 23.5	The largest city park in the nation with 5,000 acres of hiking and biking trails.	Nearly 75,000 PSU alumni live and work in the Portland metro area.	Portland is home to the legendary skate park built by skaters for skaters.	In 2004–2005, the PSU men's basketball, women's golf and women's soccer teams all won Big Sky Conference titles.	Listed by Monster.com.	

Portland State University

PROJECT:
Portland State University identity and brand redesign

DESIGN FIRM:
Sockeye Creative

LOCATION:
Portland, Oregon

CREATIVE DIRECTOR:
Peter Metz

DESIGNERS:
Erica Brinker, John Fisher, Andrew Kinzer, Peter Metz, Robert Wees

"One of the greatest things about becoming a designer in the town where you grew up is working for organizations you've always known about and teams you rooted for as a kid. You never would've imagined that one day you would rebrand them," says Peter Metz, creative director and cofounder of Sockeye Creative.

"Why do they need to be rebranded?" you might ask. Because times change.

Times have definitely changed for Portland State University. Its late arrival to the state university system and lack of university status until 1969 made it a secondary priority in Oregon's System of Higher Education for years. The university has historically been underfunded and was often thought of as a commuter school or a place where local residents could pick up a few classes part-time.

Portland State's identity was hurting. For starters, the existing logo was strictly typographic. Many critics complained that it lacked presence, that it was

PORTLAND STATE UNIVERSITY

˄ Previous logo

˄ Redesigned logo
<< Redesigned admissions brochure

˄ Redesigned logo

123

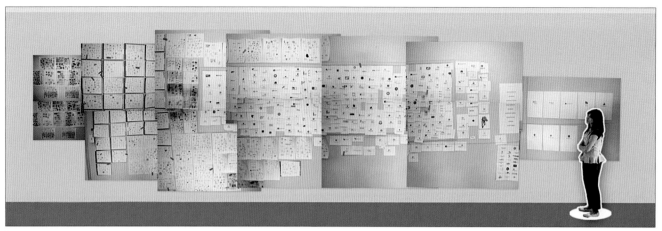

^ Sockeye Creative's logo concept wall

^ Redesigned stationery

"hardly a logo at all." Some departments minimized its visibility by relegating it to the back of collateral or removed it all together in favor of simply typesetting the university name.

To make matters worse, merchandise, branding and the individual colleges and departments were all working independently, further fragmenting the university's external visual messaging. Port-

land State didn't appear to be well connected with the city, with the students or even with itself. So, by 2006, the time had come to implement an overdue rebranding strategy that would give the university a unified look with and logo.

The primary goal of the rebrand was to create a singular identity that was more reflective of—and unique to—Portland State. The brand rollout would also include new visual guidelines to help promote the university's stronger, more unified voice.

Although nine firms competed for the business, Sockeye Creative was well positioned to give the university what it needed. One thing put it head and shoulders above the rest: Sockeye's ability to tap into clients' true voices and inspire them to expose what their brand is all about.

In the words of Julie Smith, chair of the selection committee,

"I liked how sophisticated and creative Sockeye is in discovering the 'experience' of a place and representing that 'experience' in a visually compelling way that inspires audiences."

The new visual identity package needed to communicate that Portland State was more than a typical academic experience. A lot had changed in the past fifty years. The university was growing alongside Portland and had become a hotbed for sustainability and forward thinking. Today, Portland State is the largest and most diverse university in the state system, serving more students and conferring more master's degrees annually than any other Oregon university. Its story needed to be updated.

Sockeye designers interviewed key university stakeholders and a

^ Redesigned admissions brochures

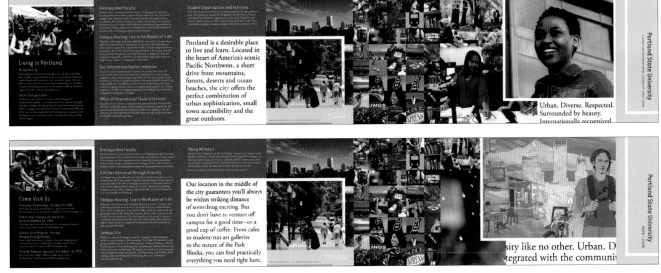

^ Redesigned admissions brochures

task force of faculty, administrators and students. Although the discussions unearthed years of spoken and hidden frustration, it also brought to light a lot of pride. By soliciting input from the greater campus community, the process was a catalyst to connectivity, which began to emerge as a central theme.

By the time the design firm's interviews were complete, a solid creative brief had been drafted to serve as the project blueprint. The design could finally begin.

The designers first focused on identifying Portland State's brand personality. Using the creative brief, six key words were selected that were communicative of Portland State and could drive the design conceptually: confident, passionate, human, urban, aspirational and connected. These important characteristics guided the design process every step of the way.

The design team knew that they didn't want the university to seem too traditional, so the logo needed to reflect that. When looking at marks from educational institutions across the globe, many common metaphors used in higher education were represented; icons like flames, books, garland and shields communicate a traditional academic experience. But they didn't begin to capture what the Portland State experience is all about. The connection to the community and the city were much more compelling and relevant for this young urban university.

The process began with five designers sketching while keeping the six key words in mind. The Sockeye Creative approach is to explore until no stone has been left unturned. The longer you are around the forms, the more you start to see hidden relationships. From abstract marks to monograms to strict logotypes, the designers tried it all.

Over four thousand sketches were generated and posted on the office wall of the firm for internal review. Painstakingly, the selection was narrowed down to twelve marks that reflected the six key words. These were presented to the task force, who chose three favorites that would be displayed publicly. Comments from the cam-

∧ Redesigned University brochure

∧ Previous University brochure

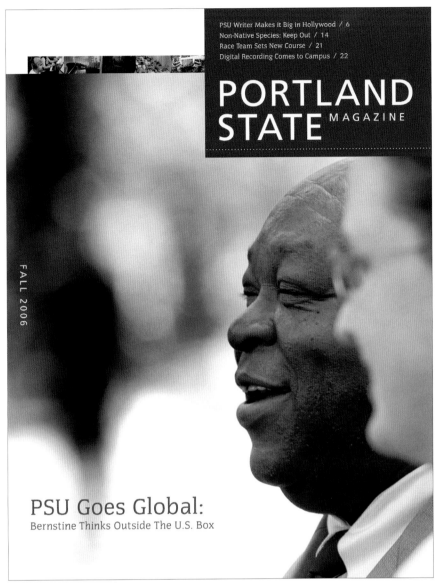

PSU Writer Makes it Big in Hollywood / 6
Non-Native Species: Keep Out / 14
Race Team Sets New Course / 21
Digital Recording Comes to Campus / 22

PORTLAND STATE MAGAZINE

FALL 2006

PSU Goes Global:
Bernstine Thinks Outside The U.S. Box

˄ Redesigned alumni magazine

˄ Previous alumni magazine

pus community were collected and considered before a single direction was chosen for refinement.

The final mark—an artful configuration of interlocking letterforms—was chosen because it accomplished many goals of the rebrand. The contemporary monogram is a nod to tradition but also acts as a testament to the university's desire to do things differently. The interweaving lines speak of connectivity and interdependence. The bold line weight and symmetrical configuration of the logomark conveys confidence.

And the fluidity and movement of the letterforms communicates sustainability.

"What the new mark does," says Cassie McVeety, vice president for university relations, "is portray that connection, which is really what makes Portland State distinct. Everything we do is tied to the community, to research, to our students."

In addition to a new brand mark, the undertaking included creating an entirely new brand platform with updated typography, color palettes, templates, website, collateral and a comprehensive brand standards guide. Each step was part of a strategic effort to cement the identity and promote the authentic PSU experience.

There has already been a tremendous amount of positive buzz and support for the new

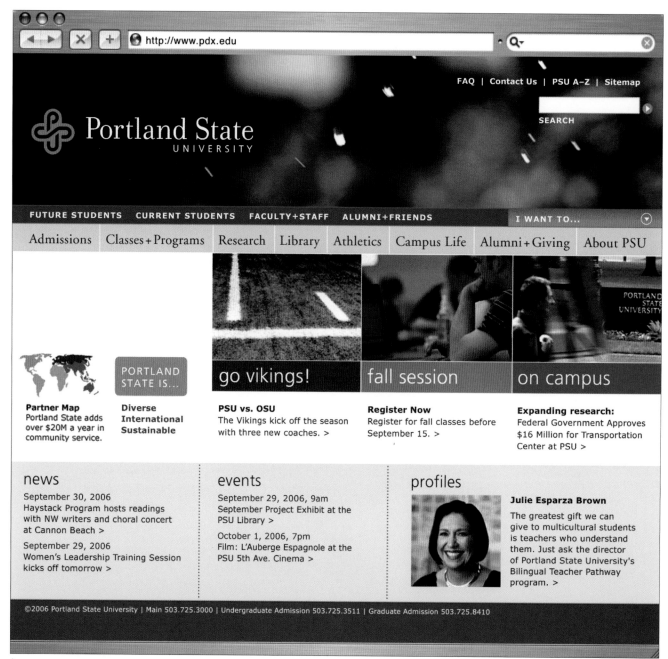

⌃ Redesigned website

mark. The story was featured on the front page of *The Oregonian*, the largest daily newspaper in the Pacific Northwest, where the reporter spoke to the significance of the university rebrand as well as its challenges.

With all the pieces of the visual identity package in place, Sockeye Creative believes the new Portland State logo is confident, bold and accomplishes the goals of the university and the design firm. The logo connects the university to its city of Portland, its students and finally, to itself.

WORDS OF WISDOM

"Besides taking into account the usual key factors that a redesign entails—goals, why the redesign is needed, audience, assessment of emotional and functional benefits, codification of the brand personality, evaluation of equity in the current identity, the marketplace and the competition—the best advice I can offer is that understanding the current audience's perception of the brand is vital to any redesign. There can be a huge disparity between what the client believes the brand is and what the audience perceives the brand to be. Naturally, one would want to retain any parts of the current brand identity (or brand identities if the reason for the redesign is a merger) that have brand value and that the audience perceives positively."

Robin Landa, Branding and Creative Strategist
New York City, New York
www.robinlanda.com

John Read
President and CEO

Outward Bound, USA
100 Mystery Point Road
Garrison, NY 10524
outwardbound.org

Tel: 845 424 4000 ext. 245
Fax: 845 424 4121
jread@outwardbound.org

OUTWARD BOUND

Changing Lives

Building Teams

Transforming Schools

OUTWARD BOUND

OUTWARD BOUND

100 Mystery Point Road
Garrison, NY 10524

OUTWARD BOUND

100 Mystery Point Road
Garrison, NY 10524

Outward Bound USA
100 Mystery Point Road, Garrison, NY 10524   Tel: 845 424 4000   Fax: 845 424 4121   outwardbound.org

Outward Bound

PROJECT:
Outward Bound brand renewal

DESIGN FIRMS:
Identityworks and
Connacher Design

LOCATIONS:
Rye, New York, and
Stamford, Connecticut

BRANDING CONSULTANT:
Tony Spaeth

DESIGN CONSULTANT:
Nat Connacher

In 2003, Tony Spaeth met Greg Farrell, president of an education reform initiative called Expeditionary Learning Outward Bound, and agreed to help Farrell address his company's identity problems. The name was cumbersome (and ELOB didn't help). More importantly, its incorporation of the parent name, Outward Bound, was a mixed blessing. The positives (awareness, authority, cultural values) were great, but its wilderness association, i.e. kids in the woods is misleading. Expeditionary Learning deals with kids in their classrooms. It is in the business of school reform, applying to the classroom environment and curriculum what has been learned in the woods about learning and personal growth via expeditions.

The ELOB issues couldn't be solved, however, without addressing the parent organization's own branding problems, including its low-visibility wordmark-in-symbol and the symbol's Victorian personality. Today's Outward Bound needs to be known as the educational force it is becoming in America's urban environments, corporate offices and schoolrooms, not just in the wilderness.

OUTWARD BOUND

Outward Bound. USA

^ Previous logo

^ Redesigned logo
<< Redesigned business card (front and back), letterhead, envelope and mailing label

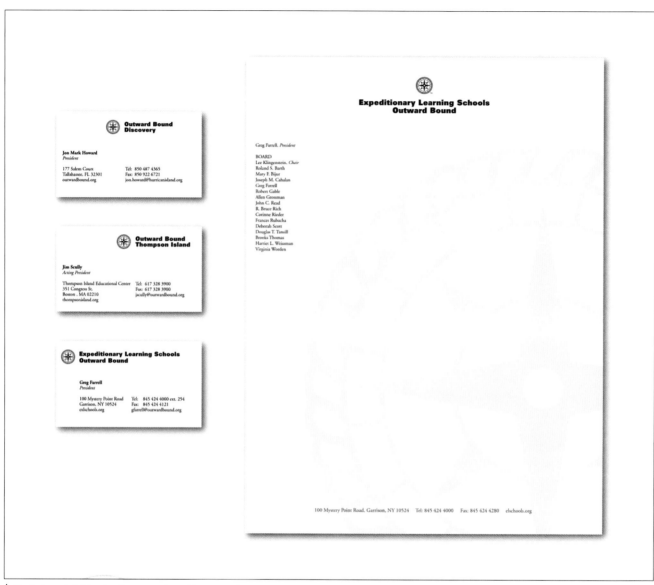

︿ Redesigned division business cards and letterhead

The compass-rose symbol had value as a seal of authenticity but was a handicap both in its technically weak branding impact and as a barrier to change.

John Read, the new leader of Outward Bound USA, quickly recognized the opportunities an identity change could offer. He was already working to transform the organization by consolidating the seven autonomous schools of Outward Bound USA into one stronger entity. In early 2005, five of the seven voted to consolidate. (The New York City and North Carolina units would continue, for the time being, under charters.)

Designer Nat Connacher joined the team. The words "Outward Bound" were separated from the compass-rose symbol so the text (the strongest brand asset) could be made bigger, and a simplified compass symbol could be used to anchor a more flexible signature system. Outward Bound Wilderness could now identify itself as one of several Outward Bound programs. Expeditionary Learning Schools could free itself of the misleading overbranding, while keeping the visual association and a more proportionate verbal association by adding the text "a Division of Outward Bound."

Division names & signatures

Expeditionary Learning Schools
Outward Bound

Outward Bound
Professional

Outward Bound
Wilderness

Outward Bound
Discovery

Affiliate, Center & Council names & signatures

Outward Bound
Baltimore Chesapeake Bay

New York City
Outward Bound

North Carolina
Outward Bound

Outward Bound
Philadelphia

Outward Bound
Atlanta

Outward Bound
Thompson Island

ʌ Redesigned division signature treatments

ʌ Redesigned T-shirt

ʌ Redesigned highway signage

ʌ Previous highway signage

ʌ Redesigned hat

breakfast,
lunch &
dinner

vegetarian
& vegan
heaven.

cocktails

outdoor patio

bocce ball

503.335.8233
3024 NE Alberta
Portland OR

breakfast,
lunch &
dinner

vegetarian
& vegan
friendly

cocktails

outdoor patio

bocce ball

503.335.8233
3024 NE Alberta
Portland OR

Vita Café

PROJECT:
Vita Café identity
and menu design

DESIGN FIRM:
FullblastInc.com

LOCATION:
Portland, Oregon

CREATIVE DIRECTOR/DESIGNER/
PHOTOGRAPHER:
N. Todd Skiles

Vita Café had been in business for six years with no real identity. As an alternative vegan/vegetarian restaurant, it produced all of its menus and graphics in-house. The eating establishment is situated in a transition neighborhood with a loyal following from a variety of groups: vegetarians, vegans, local bike messengers, the gay and lesbian community, hippies, young hipsters, politically/environmentally active groups and others.

When the new owners chose to have an identity designed, they hired FullblastInc.com.

One of the major challenges was that the existing clientele and staff would most likely resist a new identity (or changed identity of any kind), so it was imperative to capture the alternative feel of the restaurant and not veer in a corporate direction.

FullblastInc.com's solution was the development of a logotype (distressed type) combined with a distressed icon that was photographed from an inside wall of the eating establishment. The menu's imagery included high-contrast photographs of the restaurant and the neighborhood. The primary images are of the facade of the building in black (top) and a detail of the table setting in red (knife and fork crossing themselves).

All paper used in the printing of items was 100 percent recycled and chlorine free.

There was nothing but positive feedback from the staff and clientele. Some even e-mailed FullblastInc.com directly, complimenting the designer on the new menus.

∧ Redesigned logo
<< Redesigned postcards

∧ Previous logo

^ Redesigned menu cover

^ Previous menu cover

^ Previous menu page

^ Redesigned menu

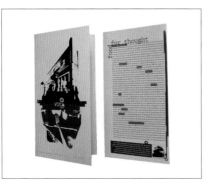

^ Redesigned menu

dinner

STARTERS	sm/lg
MEDITERRANEAN PLATTER	8.5
hummus, marinated olives, cucumbers, roasted peppers and warmed pita	
SPICY TEMPEH STICKS	7
battered and deep fried organic tempeh with Thai peanut dipping sauce	
VEGAN NACHOS	7.5
tortilla chips topped with beans, brown rice, black olives, salsa, guacamole and vegan 'cheese' sauce	
FRESH CUT FRIES	2.5 / 4
~ add spice +.75	
BISCUITS AND GRAVY	3/ 5
almond gravy over homemade biscuits	
THE 'HOG'	3/ 5
almond gravy over homemade herb and onion bread	

BURGERS

~ vegan veggie burger
~ or free range, hormone free quarter pound beef

BASIC BURGER	5
~ add cheese +1	
~ add tempeh 'fakin' or peppered-bacon +1	
MUSHROOM AND ONION BURGER	6.5
~ add blue cheese +1	
CHILI BURGER	7
topped with 3 bean chili and grilled onions	
JIMBO BURGER	7
topped with a fried free range egg and peppered-bacon	

SOUPS AND SALADS	sm/lg
THAI COCONUT SOUP	3.5/5
served with our homemade herb and onion bread	
3 BEAN VEGETARIAN CHILI	4.5/6
served with a sweet corn muffin	
~ add cheese, onion or sour cream +.5	
DAILY HOMEMADE SOUP	3.5/5
served with our homemade herb and onion bread	
MIXED GREENS SALAD	3.5/6.5
organic greens, cucumber, tomatoes and sunflower seeds	
~ add baked wild salmon +3	
CAESAR SALAD	3.5/6.5
served with our homemade vegan Caesar dressing	
~ add baked wild salmon +3	
GREEK SALAD	3.75/6.75
crumbled feta cheese, roasted red peppers, cucumber, tomatoes, red onion, kalamata olives with basil vinaigrette	
~ add organic tempeh fried or sautéed +2	
FRIED CHICKPEA SALAD	6.75
fried chickpeas with tomatoes, basil and corn over organic greens	
ASIAN CHOPPED SALAD	6.75
cucumber, red peppers, edamame, soy nuts, wasabi-seasoned peas and organic greens with orange miso dressing	
SOUP AND SALAD	7.5
any soup and salad served with homemade herb and onion bread	

DRESSINGS:
Lemon Tahini, Orange Miso, Basil Vinaigrette,
Honey Dijon, Ranch, Blue Cheese, Vegan 1000 Island

^ Redesigned menu page

^ Redesigned menu page

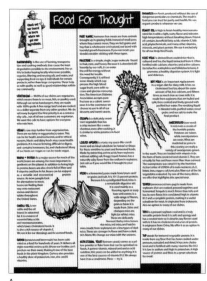

^ Previous menu page

WASHINGTON CONSERVATION GUILD

WASHINGTON CONSERVATION GUILD

PO Box 23364 | Washington, DC 20026

WASHINGTON CONSERVATION GUILD

Mail PO Box 23364 | Washington, DC 20026
Email wcg@washingtonconservationguild.org
Web www.washingtonconservationguild.org

The **Washington Conservation Guild** is a nonprofit organization of conservation professionals, founded in 1967 and based in Washington, D.C., U.S.A. The Guild serves as an information exchange for members, and as a resource to the general public for learning about the care of their personal collections.

Mail PO Box 23364 | Washington, DC 20026 | **Email** wcg@washingtonconservationguild.org | **Web** www.washingtonconservationguild.org

Washington Conservation Guild

PROJECT:

Washington Conservation
Guild identity redesign

DESIGN FIRM:

CC Graphic Design

LOCATION:

Salt Lake City, Utah

CREATIVE DIRECTOR/DESIGNER:

Carolyn Crowley

The Washington Conservation Guild is a nonprofit organization of conservation professionals, based in Washington, DC. While serving primarily as a forum for the exchange of information among its members, the Guild also seeks to help nonconservators learn more about caring for their own art and artifacts. The ideas the organization wanted to communicate through its image included professionalism, clarity, tradition yet innovation and a focus on Washington DC, which is well known for its museums and where the Guild's central office is located. The client's previous logo and identity was executed poorly and did not convey any sense of modernity or new ideas.

The idea for the new logo and identity was to use three rectangles, arranged as panels on display in a museum. Each rectangle framed each of the initial letters of the organization's name. The new design redrew the image of the capitol building and kept the focus on the initials WCG so that there was some connection to the client's old identity. The logo was created in one color to keep the organization's costs down for printed materials. The blue, PMS 285, and the font Cochin were chosen to portray the organization as young, vibrant, yet traditional and classic.

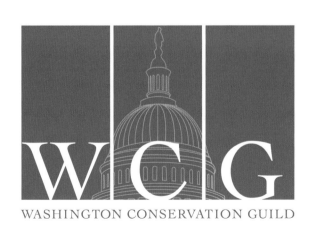

^ Redesigned logo
<< Redesigned stationery

^ Previous logo

★
JOFFREY
BALLET

70 EAST LAKE STREET, SUITE 1300
CHICAGO IL 60601-5917

NON-PROFIT ORG.
U.S. POSTAGE
PAID
CHICAGO, IL
PERMIT NO. 4286

INNOVATION. INSPIRATION. ARTISTRY.

2004-2005 SEASON

SUBSCRIBE
AND SEE

A NUREYEV TRIBUTE

AMERICAN MASTERWORKS

ACCENT ARPINO

+

AVAILABLE NOW,
ONLY TO SUBCRIBERS

THE NUTCRACKER

BALANCHINE CENTENNIAL
CELEBRATION

The Joffrey Ballet is Chicago's own world-class American ballet company committed to bringing energetic and unique ballet performances to audiences here and throughout the world. In 2004-2005, The Joffrey Ballet will present a diverse repertoire honoring master choreographers Robert Joffrey, Gerald Arpino, George Balanchine, Jerome Robbins and Paul Taylor. You'll enjoy Russian Diaghilev-era performances, original folk dance interpretations, American cutting-edge modern master-pieces, and your timeless favorites Stravinsky, Vivaldi, Tchaikovsky and Mahler to name a few. Experience the energy, entertainment and special benefits of the season by becoming a Joffrey Ballet subscriber today!

SUBSCRIPTIONS
START AT $50!

Joffrey Ballet

PROJECT:
Joffrey Ballet rebranding

DESIGN FIRM:
Avenue Marketing
& Communications

LOCATION:
Chicago, Illinois

For years, red ink was flowing at the Joffrey Ballet, Chicago's own world-class American ballet. The Joffrey needed to increase awareness, clarify its image and reputation, and most importantly, fill seats at performances.

It was a challenge. As a non-profit organization, the Joffrey has very limited budgets, and ballet is not a high-demand entertainment option for most people. Previous advertising efforts had focused on emphasizing the athleticism of the dancers coupled with a marketing strategy broadly positioned at the general public.

Avenue's initial research proved that profitability didn't lie in trying to convert average Joes to attend the ballet. The performing arts organization was competing with movies, restaurants, sports, music and other options for the audience's entertainment dollars.

Instead, they identified the core Joffrey Ballet patrons and patrons of the arts as the highest priority target audience. Focusing on this audience helped Avenue identify the attributes that make the Joffrey Ballet unique: artistry, inspiration and energy. These insights drove a new approach to marketing that emphasizes a narrow focus on targeting and converting the "dormant ballet and art patron" versus the masses.

The rebranding included a comprehensive new identity based on a star icon. Perfect, consistent and inspirational in character, the star is associated with many positive connotations and possibilities.

JOFFREY
BALLET

JOFFREY

ʌ Previous logo

ʌ Redesigned logo
<<Redesigned subscription brochure cover

∧ Redesigned subscription brochure page

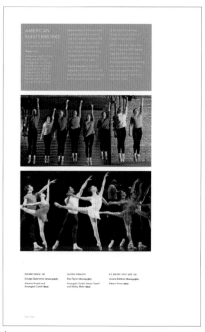

∧ Redesigned subscription brochure page

∧ Redesigned subscription brochure page

↑ Redesigned subscription brochure page

Photography and color were also integral elements. Guidelines were created for new photography characterized by artistic body formations and geometric or grid patterns. A sophisticated, neutral, supporting color palette underscored the dramatic new photography.

Previous marketing materials that emphasized athleticism and were cluttered with design elements and information were completely redesigned to play up clean sophistication and beauty. The new materials captured the inspiration and artistry of the performances, and made ordering tickets much easier for patrons.

The Joffrey implemented many operational improvements, including new repertoires, schedules, revised pricing and an overhaul of the media plan, which helped support the new brand and marketing rollout.

Today, ticket sales are rising, profits are back and reserves are increasing. Performance revenues are up 19 percent, full-season sales are 27 percent ahead of last year, and subscription renewal rates are up to 75 percent from 50 percent four years ago. Corporate donations are up 73 percent, and foundation donations are up 88 percent.

Additionally, the Joffrey Ballet has received extensive media coverage, including articles in *The Wall Street Journal* and *Chicago Crain's*

Magazine, and it was named one of the top fifty marketers by *Advertising Age*. James Newcomb, senior manager of corporate identity and sponsorship for Chicago-based Boeing Co., was recently quoted in *Chicago Crain's Magazine* as saying, "The Joffrey is the best-case current example of arts marketing right now."

Hope Wolman, director of marketing and public relations at the Joffrey, sums up the positive change, "The impact of the rebranding has exceeded our wildest imagination. We came to Avenue looking for a new logo, but they have given us a brand that creates passion and desire."

ʌ Redesigned 50th anniversary subscription brochure pages

ʌ Redesigned 50th anniversary subscription brochure cover

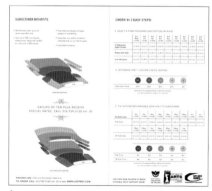

ʌ Redesigned 50th anniversary subscription brochure pages

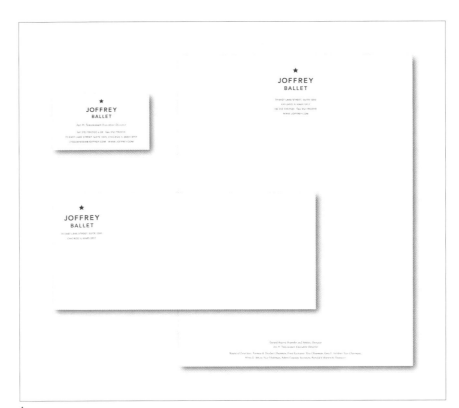

^ Redesigned stationery

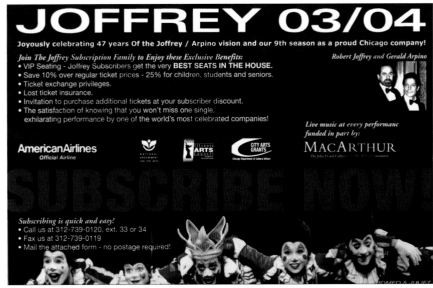

^ Previous subscription graphics

^ Previous subscription graphics

^ Previous PR kit label

^ Previous mailer cover

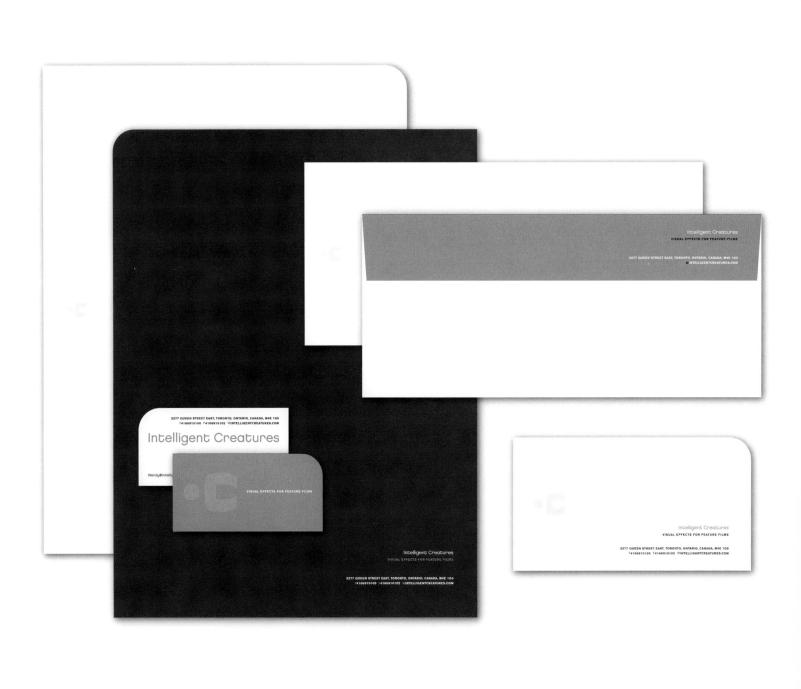

Intelligent Creatures

PROJECT:

Intelligent Creatures identity

DESIGN FIRM:

3 Dogz Creative Inc.

LOCATION:

Toronto, Ontario, Canada

CREATIVE DIRECTORS:

Dave Gouveia, Chris Elkerton, Roberta Judge

DESIGNER:

Ryan Broadbent

Intelligent Creatures is a visual effects company based in Toronto, Canada, working primarily in the feature film industry. They also provide services such as animation, compositing, design and on-set supervision with advanced technologies. 3 Dogz Creative began working with them at their inception, helping to develop an identity for the new company. Too much input from the partners and other initial frustrations led to a mark that, although very popular internally, didn't seem to brand the company properly.

In early 2005, the company approached 3 Dogz Creative for a fresh look, wanting the firm's ideas and rationales for what they thought would reflect Intelligent Creatures best. The business wanted their new mark to have the weight and seriousness of companies in the same industry. The image had to be simple, yet strong, and easily recognized on movie sets.

3 Dogz Creative presented several new designs, ranging from simple wordmarks to elaborate marks and graphics. However, the design all partners in the firm gravitated towards, and the favorite of the design team, was a simple, stylized version of the IC letterforms, which had the feel of a creature. The process continued with tweaking and perfecting the shapes. In the end, Intelligent Creatures' request was achieved: a simple, strong mark, easily recognized on movie sets.

The shape of the new mark was introduced in subtle ways to the corporate pocket folder, the stationery and the client's new website. The mark has now become part of all merchandising, including hats and T-shirts.

^ Redesigned logo

<< Redesigned stationery package

^ Previous logo

831 42ND STREET • DES MOINES, IOWA 50312 • PHONE 515 277 6261 • TOLL FREE 877 862 5621 • FAX 515 277 8019

831 42nd STREET
DES MOINES, IOWA 50312

lbakros@dmplayhouse.com

LEE ANN BAKROS
Communications Director/
Group Sales Director

TOLL FREE 877 862 5621
PHONE 515 974 5358
ADMIN FAX 515 271 8080

WWW.DMPLAYHOUSE.COM

WWW.DMPLAYHOUSE.COM

The Des Moines Playhouse

PROJECT:
The Des Moines
Playhouse identity

DESIGN FIRM:
Sayles Graphic Design

LOCATION:
Des Moines, Iowa

ART DIRECTOR/DESIGNER:
John Sayles

The Des Moines Playhouse is among the six oldest continuously operating community theatres in the United States, but until recently, its history, rich with community enhancement and national recognition, was far more recognizable than the identity of the playhouse itself. After eighty-seven years, the Des Moines Playhouse had fallen victim to an unidentifiable visual image. Each brochure and promotional piece looked as though it were designed by a different designer—because that is exactly what had happened. The result was a hodgepodge of imagery and an inconsistent look.

Sayles Graphic Design was selected to design a cohesive identity for the Playhouse and remind the residents of Des Moines that the theatre was still a fun place to come for quality entertainment. The challenge began with a brainstorming session involving both the team at Sayles and the Playhouse. Following several fact-finding and brainstorming sessions, the Sayles team developed "Play your part" as the season's tagline.

Every part of the campaign was consistent, from the sizes of the

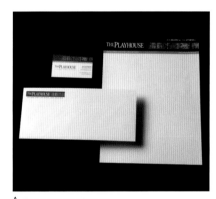

^ Previous stationery

^ Redesigned logo
<< Redesigned letterhead (front and back), envelope, and business card (front and back)

^ Previous logo

brochures to the colors used on the different pieces. Traditional theatre symbols, such as tickets and director's hands, were used, while steering clear of cliché.

Ʌ Redesigned rack brochure front

Ʌ Previous collateral

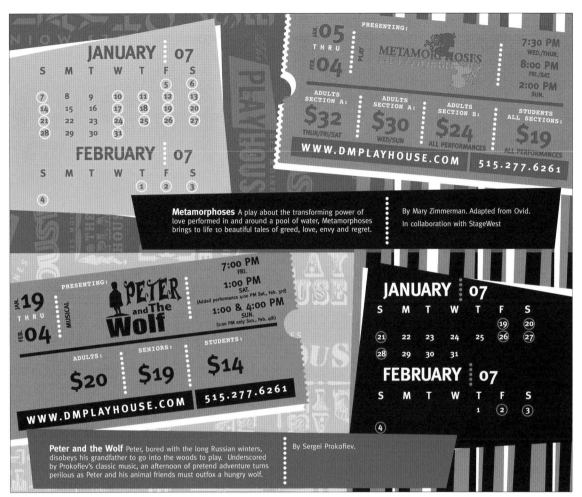

^ Redesigned rack brochure back

WORDS OF WISDOM

"Hire the designer that you feel comfortable with, who is willing to truly listen to you. Explain your expectations, in deliverables and time. Pay more than you want to. It's worth it."

Sean Adams
AdamsMorioka, Inc.
Beverly Hills, California
www.adamsmorioka.com

CENTRAL FLORIDA WEST

CAROLYN MATHIESON
Vice President

T: 352-536-2047 | F: 352-536-1171
Cell: 321-243-9271
Email: cpmathieson@yahoo.com
12914 South Highway 27 | Clermont, Florida 34711

CENTRAL FLORIDA WEST

12914 SOUTH HIGHWAY 27 • CLERMONT, FLORIDA 34711
T: 352-526-2047 • F: 352-536-1171

CENTRAL FLORIDA WEST

12914 SOUTH HIGHWAY 27 • CLERMONT, FLORIDA 34711

Central Florida West

PROJECT:
CFWest identity redesign

DESIGN FIRM:
Advertising By Design

LOCATION:
Clermont, Florida

CREATIVE DIRECTOR/DESIGNER:
Dawn Burgess

When the new marketing director of a family-owned real estate firm approached Advertising by Design, the firm's primary focus was land investment, entitlements and approvals. With immediate plans to enter into vertical commercial construction—such as shopping centers and professional office space—the business required a new graphic image to level the playing field in a very competitive local market. The client requested an identity system that was polished enough to appeal to white-collar professionals, including buyers, investors and developers. After many concepts and meetings to further develop scope, it was decided to change the name to Central Florida West—which zeroed in on the exact location of the properties under development.

The final design sprang forth from this new direction. The designer shortened the name further to simply "CFWest." It not only looked better but also rolls off the tongue easier. The stylized compass with the west arm highlighted enhanced the overall meaning. The new brand concept also allows enough flexibility to introduce additional division identities should projects take the business to other geographical areas within Central Florida—such as East, North or South. The launch of the identity was to a very tight niche market, where it successfully garnered instant attention. The identity is used primarily for site signage and client-generated proposals, as well as a complete stationery system.

^ Previous logo

^ Redesigned logo

<< Redesigned business card (front and back), letterhead and stationery

union square PARTNERSHIP

Union Square Partnership

PROJECT:
Union Square Partnership
identity redesign

DESIGN FIRM:
Shapiro Design Associates Inc.

LOCATION:
Irvington, NY

ART DIRECTOR/DESIGNER:
Ellen Shapiro

Union Square—centered at the intersection of 14th Street, Park Avenue South and Broadway—is one of the fastest growing, most rapidly changing neighborhoods in New York City. A few decades ago it was home to fading department and discount stores, seedy bars and a run-down park. Now it is home to some of Manhattan's most trendy restaurants, clubs and shops, new luxury housing, a beautifully renovated park—with fabulous Greenmarket—and vastly upgraded subway station, a transportation nexus.

In 2005, the 14th Street Union Square Business Improvement District renamed itself Union Square Partnership to communicate the expansion of the neighborhood (it goes far beyond

ʌ Redesigned logo

<<Redesigned presentation cover folder design

ʌ Previous logo applications

14th Street) and a vibrant new civic-business partnership.

Shapiro Design Associates Inc., was commissioned to design a new logo for use on everything from signage, letterhead, website, and event invitations to trash cans and patches on sanitation workers' uniforms.

In establishing goals for the identity redesign, Ellen Shapiro determined that the logo needed to be evocative of the diverse, fun, hip, friendly, young, colorful and happening neighborhood. The designer, who had lived in the neighborhood for ten years, explored a number of typographic ideas, including a green *u* surrounded by the brick of the buildings around the park; an *un sq*, sort of like the *un-cola*; and a mosaic square with a subtle *14*.

The concept selected by Union Square Partnership executive director Karen Shaw and her team was the *u* linked with the square, with a bit of a twist. It suggests both the young, chic vibe of the neighborhood and the business-civic partnership of the organization.

The next design phase involved a close look at various color explorations and type treatments with the *un-sq* mark. Because Union Square Partnership is a business organization, the team opted for typography with a corporate feel.

ʌ Proposed street banner

ʌ Proposed street banner

With an eye toward the budgets of the many printed pieces it would produce each year, they chose a two-color color scheme: bright blue with a grassy green.

Shapiro Design designed stationery, business cards and signs, and demonstrated the new logo in context of typical applications, including press kit folders and street banners.

⋏ Identity explorations

WORDS OF WISDOM

"Don't—in an effort to 'redesign' or 'change' an organization—do so without great care in regards to its history and potential equity. Too often, we as designers jump in, optimistic about the opportunity, and fail to consider that there is much more to a company than its logo. We must be aware that change for the pure sake of change—without careful consideration of the audience, the impetus or the possible equity the company may have in its existing identity—could actually hurt that company and its brand image, resulting in a negative impact on the company itself."

Mark E. Sackett
Reflectur (formerly Sackett Design)
San Francisco/Los Angeles/New York
www.reflectur.com

Schellin Grounds Maintenance
195 N Hickory Ridge Drive
Port Clinton, OH 43452

419.797.9068 *phone*

Brad Schellin *owner*

Schellin Grounds Maintenance
195 N Hickory Ridge Drive
Port Clinton, OH 43452

419.797.9068 *phone*

Enhancing and maintaining your outdoor spaces

Enhancing and maintaining your outdoor spaces

Schellin Grounds Maintenance

PROJECT:
SgM logo and stationery system

DESIGN FIRM:
angryporcupine*design

LOCATION:
Park City, Utah

ART DIRECTOR/DESIGNER:
Cheryl Roder-Quill

Schellin Grounds Maintenance (SgM), founded fifteen years ago by owner Brad Schellin, is an established lawn maintenance and landscaping company located in northern Ohio. SgM offers a variety of multi-seasonal services including lawn care, landscaping, snowplowing and spring/fall cleanup (weeding, trimming, mulching and more).

Known for its outstanding customer service, dependability and reliability, the company has seen considerable growth in the past few years and is beginning to offer additional services to meet the ever-growing needs of its customers. SgM's logo was developed fifteen years ago, so the company was ready for a new

identity that would reflect the evolution of the company, the services it provides and its commitment to the community.

In 2006, Schellin Grounds Maintenance asked angryporcupine* design to develop a new logo/identity solution that would grow with the company, be unique within

^ Previous logo

^ Redesigned logo

<<Redesigned business card (front and back) and letterhead

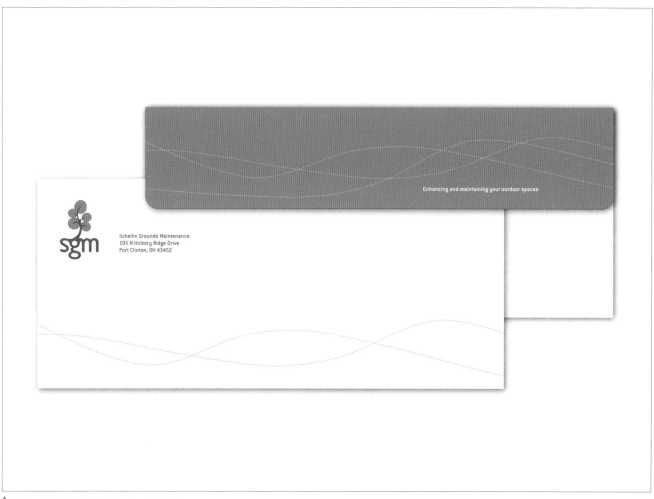

^ Redesigned envelope (front and back)

Schellin Grounds Maintenance
195 N Hickory Ridge Drive
Port Clinton, OH 43452

Enhancing and maintaining your outdoor spaces

the industry, imply both corporate strength and personalized focus, suggest a mature (yet growing) company, be stable and rooted within the community and communicate with at-a-glance simplicity to a specific target audience.

Initial brainstorming generated dozens of possibilities. The client suggested keywords that best describe the company and its services for use in this initial ideation phase. These keywords included:

- dependable
- friendly
- quality
- trusted
- flexible
- upscale

angryporcupine*design developed a logo/identity solution that represents the evolution of this mature, established lawn maintenance and landscaping company. The roots of the tree form the company initials and suggest trust and dependability. The final colors, PMS 377 (green) and PMS 154 (brown), reflect the nature of the client's business. The tree foliage is aligned in such a manner as to suggest growth. The solution is friendly, approachable and reflects the commitment of the

∧ Previous letterhead, envelope and business card

client to outstanding customer service. The new logo and identity system components are distinctive and deliver a successful solution for this growing company.

WORDS OF WISDOM

"Rebranding may be the single most cost-effective thing you can do as an organization's leader to effect desired change. Therefore, make sure your designer sees the organization in your mind, the one you're working to build, so that design can help you build it."

Tony Spaeth
Identityworks
Rye, New York
www.identityworks.com

Energias de Portugal

PROJECT:
EDP identity

DESIGN FIRM:
MyBrand

LOCATION:
Lisbon, Portugal

ART DIRECTOR:
Rui Roquete

DESIGNERS:
This was a teamwork project.

The integration of thirteen separate regional businesses resulted in Energias de Portugal (EDP) in 1976. EDP long enjoyed a monopolistic position for the supply of electricity across Portugal, yet with market liberalization it started to face the challenge of competition. This required it to do more to attract and retain its customers, a goal hindered by its brand reputation as a distant and impenetrable bureaucracy. EDP recognized a clear and urgent need to transform its brand reputation and to create a higher performance, customer-focused business.

MyBrand defined a brand position based on the idea of "nearness," underpinned by the brand values of simplicity, confidence and social responsibility. The brand position and brand values guided the creative development of EDP's core brand communications, which are captured in the energetic, warm smile that forms their brand mark: a sincere, spontaneous and friendly human gesture that projects EDP's customer service ambitions and provokes business change. It also contrasts markedly with their previous symbol: a blue turbine.

The initial results were remarkable. Portuguese consumers were fast to recognize the new brand as a clean break with the past—"a smile for everyone"—and firmly took on board the clear message that the business would deliver substantial change.

^ Previous logo

^ Redesigned logo

<< Redesigned vehicle signage, brochure covers, storefront signage and client guide

CANTON
CROSSING

3301 Boston Street
Baltimore, Maryland 21224

P 410.558.4253

CANTONCROSSING.COM

CANTON
CROSSING

EDWIN F. HALE, SR. *Owner*

3301 Boston Street
Baltimore, Maryland 21224

P 410.558.4253

CANTONCROSSING.COM

CANTON
CROSSING

WWW.CANTONCROSSING.COM

 CANTON
CROSSING

3301 Boston Street
Baltimore, Maryland 21224

Canton Crossing

PROJECT:
Canton Crossing
identity redesign

DESIGN FIRM:
Round2 Communications

LOCATION:
Baltimore, Maryland

ART DIRECTOR:
David Taub

DESIGNER:
Glenn Villegas

Canton Crossing is a progressive mixed-use community in a booming Baltimore neighborhood along the Baltimore Harbor. At Canton Crossing, sixty-five acres of under-utilized industrial waterfront property are being revitalized into a thriving new mecca, complete with more than 1.25 million square feet of office and retail space, a luxury hotel and condominiums with breathtaking harbor views. The recently completed seventeen-story 1st Mariner Bank office tower will peer over a waterfront promenade lined with markets, shops, cafés and fine restaurants out to the marina pier that connects Canton Crossing with the harbor and beyond.

The new mark is formed by two Cs, representing the site's name. The interlocking nature of the mark creates an impression of both the sky and the water, evoking the harbor environment of Canton. The two letters are encapsulated, suggesting a point of intersection or a crossing.

A bold logo mark was required to convey the grandeur of the site and magnitude of the project. The Canton Crossing redevelopment project was designed to provide a place to live, work and play that would complement the natural maritime surroundings. Round2 employed the wave concept because waves represent a powerful force of change that continually embrace their environment. Despite its urban setting,

^ Previous logo

^ Redesigned logo

<<Redesigned stationery package

Canton Crossing is all about the peaceful, fresh and clean nature of its location. Within the logo, the soft curves and motion of the waves intersect the circle to define the air and sea, evoking soothing feelings and wholesomeness. The blues selected suggest a fresh and contemporary feeling and maintain the nautical theme, which is Canton Crossing's primary asset.

The logo mark was designed with a sense of directness and sophistication to appeal to a corporate audience, while maintaining a humanistic feel that's inviting to potential residents. The Futura font communicates elegant corporate sophistication, while remaining modern and stylish enough to convey that Canton Crossing is an attractive a place to live. The generous space between the letterforms suggests the openness of this mixed-use residential community. The juxtaposition of the dark blue and light blue, while evoking the meeting of sea and sky, also reflects the interplay of corporate and consumer modes.

Round2 recognized that though the original logo worked within the community, innovative branding strategy would be required for Canton Crossing to augment the brand's visibility among older or more established brands. Round2 extended the Canton Crossing brand with a secondary mark called Canton USA. The Canton USA mark, which shares conceptual continuity with the primary mark, represents all of the positive aspects of Canton life and its urban renaissance, with Canton Crossing as the epicenter of this progressive development. This mark allowed the client to not only strengthen the brand of the current project but to take brand ownership of the entire area and the development movement there. This brand ownership could then be leveraged to create a leadership position in a market with many strong competitors.

^ Redesigned secondary logos

^ Redesigned Canton, USA logos

^ Redesigned Canton, USA secondary logos

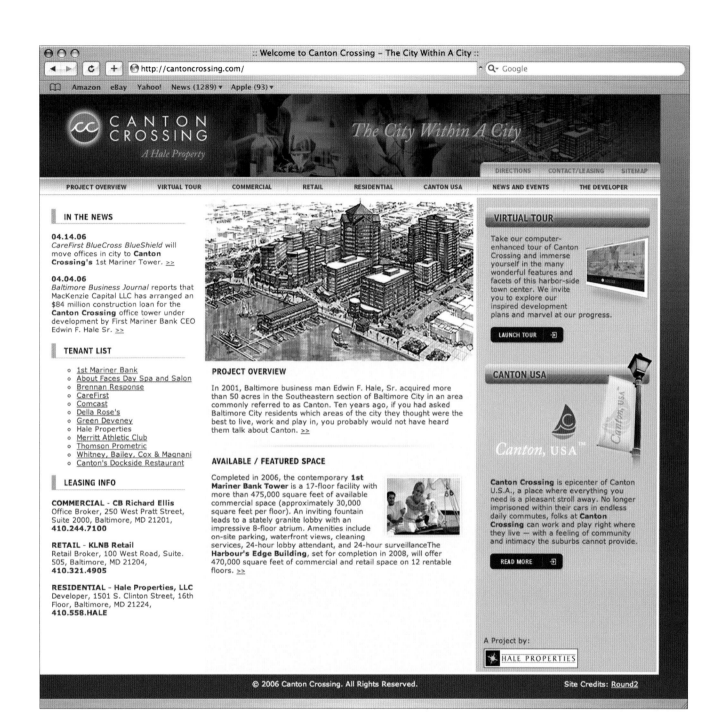

http://cantoncrossing.com/   Google

Amazon   eBay   Yahoo!   News (1289) ▾   Apple (93) ▾

CANTON CROSSING
A Hale Property

The City Within A City

DIRECTIONS   CONTACT/LEASING   SITEMAP

PROJECT OVERVIEW   VIRTUAL TOUR   COMMERCIAL   RETAIL   RESIDENTIAL   CANTON USA   NEWS AND EVENTS   THE DEVELOPER

IN THE NEWS

04.14.06
CareFirst BlueCross BlueShield will move offices in city to **Canton Crossing's** 1st Mariner Tower. >>

04.04.06
Baltimore Business Journal reports that MacKenzie Capital LLC has arranged an $84 million construction loan for the **Canton Crossing** office tower under development by First Mariner Bank CEO Edwin F. Hale Sr. >>

TENANT LIST

- 1st Mariner Bank
- About Faces Day Spa and Salon
- Brennan Response
- CareFirst
- Comcast
- Della Rose's
- Green Deveney
- Hale Properties
- Merritt Athletic Club
- Thomson Prometric
- Whitney, Bailey, Cox & Magnani
- Canton's Dockside Restaurant

LEASING INFO

COMMERCIAL - CB Richard Ellis
Office Broker, 250 West Pratt Street, Suite 2000, Baltimore, MD 21201, **410.244.7100**

RETAIL - KLNB Retail
Retail Broker, 100 West Road, Suite. 505, Baltimore, MD 21204, **410.321.4905**

RESIDENTIAL - Hale Properties, LLC
Developer, 1501 S. Clinton Street, 16th Floor, Baltimore, MD 21224, **410.558.HALE**

PROJECT OVERVIEW

In 2001, Baltimore business man Edwin F. Hale, Sr. acquired more than 50 acres in the Southeastern section of Baltimore City in an area commonly referred to as Canton. Ten years ago, if you had asked Baltimore City residents which areas of the city they thought were the best to live, work and play in, you probably would not have heard them talk about Canton. >>

AVAILABLE / FEATURED SPACE

Completed in 2006, the contemporary **1st Mariner Bank Tower** is a 17-floor facility with more than 475,000 square feet of available commercial space (approximately 30,000 square feet per floor). An inviting fountain leads to a stately granite lobby with an impressive 8-floor atrium. Amenities include on-site parking, waterfront views, cleaning services, 24-hour lobby attendant, and 24-hour surveillance. The **Harbour's Edge Building**, set for completion in 2008, will offer 470,000 square feet of commercial and retail space on 12 rentable floors. >>

VIRTUAL TOUR

Take our computer-enhanced tour of Canton Crossing and immerse yourself in the many wonderful features and facets of this harbor-side town center. We invite you to explore our inspired development plans and marvel at our progress.

LAUNCH TOUR

CANTON USA

Canton, USA™

Canton Crossing is epicenter of Canton U.S.A., a place where everything you need is a pleasant stroll away. No longer imprisoned within their cars in endless daily commutes, folks at **Canton Crossing** can work and play right where they live — with a feeling of community and intimacy the suburbs cannot provide.

READ MORE

A Project by:

HALE PROPERTIES

Site Credits: Round2

˄ Redesigned home page

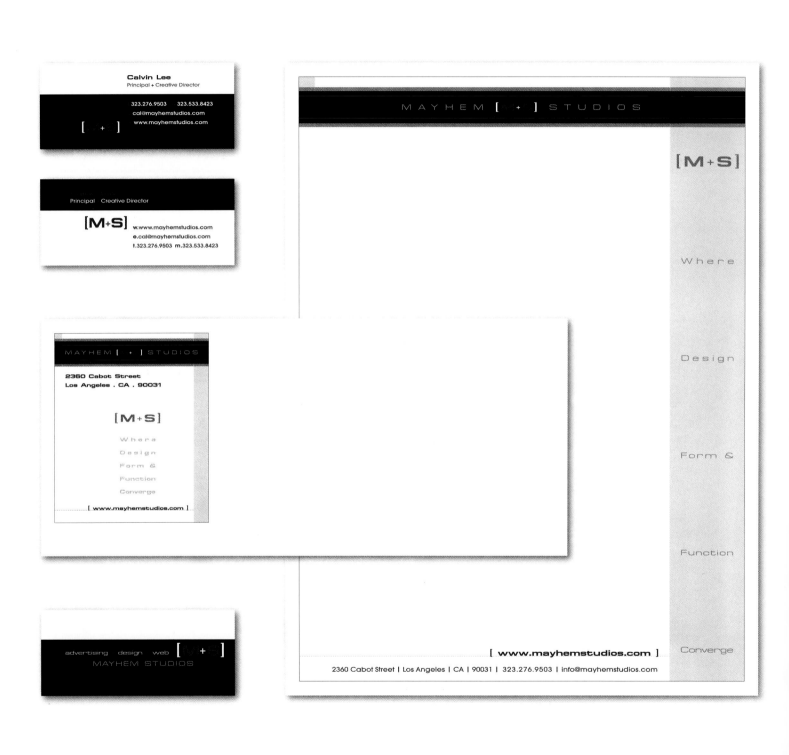

Mayhem Studios

PROJECT:

Mayhem Studios identity

DESIGN FIRM:

Mayhem Studios

LOCATION:

Los Angeles, California

ART DIRECTOR/DESIGNER:

Calvin Lee

Mayhem Studios is a small design firm that develops identity and brand recognition materials for small and large businesses across the nation. In deciding to rebrand the firm's dated look, the goal was to present a corporate, simple and clean look that conveyed trust. The new look would be carried over into the collateral, logo, website, brochure, business cards, stationery, forms, shipping labels and other firm materials.

The challenge in updating one's own identity is in treating it like any other project, without getting hung up on making it perfect. Still, attempting to convey a message representing communication and trust is a very personal project.

The original identity was an idea from one of designer Clavin Lee's past school projects. His satisfaction with that project led him to believe that the design would be useful in a future project at some point. That project turned into the original Mayhem Studios identity. Even with its bold red and black color combination, however, it seemed a little too plain.

The redesign has the same basic elements, only punched up a bit. The designer used a bolder font with a deeper red, black, and white. Setting the logo on a black background along with the company name makes the identity more striking and memorable, while showing strength and stability as a unit—and as a company.

^ Redesigned logo

^ Redesigned logo

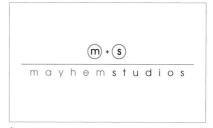

^ Previous logo

^ Redesigned logo

<<Redesigned business card (front and back), letterhead and envelope

∧ Redesigned website

∧ Redesigned website

∧ Previous website

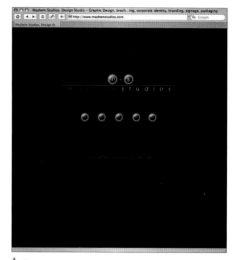

∧ Previous website

WORDS OF WISDOM

"Do your research in selecting a designer that you feel is the right fit for your business. Trust your gut instincts in making such decisions. Allow your designer the space and time to provide you good possible solutions to your business's identity crisis."

Jeff Fisher
Jeff Fisher LogoMotives
Portland, Oregon
www.jfisherlogomotives.com

Vancouver Aquarium

PROJECT:
Vancouver Aquarium
identity system

DESIGN FIRM:
Subplot Design Inc.

LOCATION:
Vancouver, British
Columbia, Canada

ART DIRECTORS:
Roy White, Matthew Clark

DESIGNERS:
Matthew Clark, Roy White,
Steph Gibson

With its fiftieth anniversary in view, the Vancouver Aquarium paused to consider its logo, which for more than thirty-five years featured a killer whale—a distinctive symbol for the aquarium as one of the first institutions to have ever displayed them. While the aquarium remains at the forefront of wild killer whale research and conservation today, management felt the killer whale no longer best represented the experience of visiting the aquarium nor the broad scope of the aquarium's programs.

The Vancouver Aquarium's fundamental purpose as an organization is aquatic conservation. The client envisions a future in which people and aquatic ecosystems live in balance, contributing to the health and well-being of each other. The Vancouver Aquarium wanted its new logo to be distinctive, contemporary and appropriate to the spirit of the organization, which offers an unforgettable aquatic experience for visitors while acting as a leader in education, conservation and marine science. It also wanted the logo to symbolize the aquarium's

commitment to all marine life (not just killer whales), and reflect the values of balance, sustainability and conservation.

Subplot Design determined that there was also a need for an overall visual identity system—a

^ Logo design process

^ Redesigned logo
<< Redesigned aquarium exterior

^ Previous logo

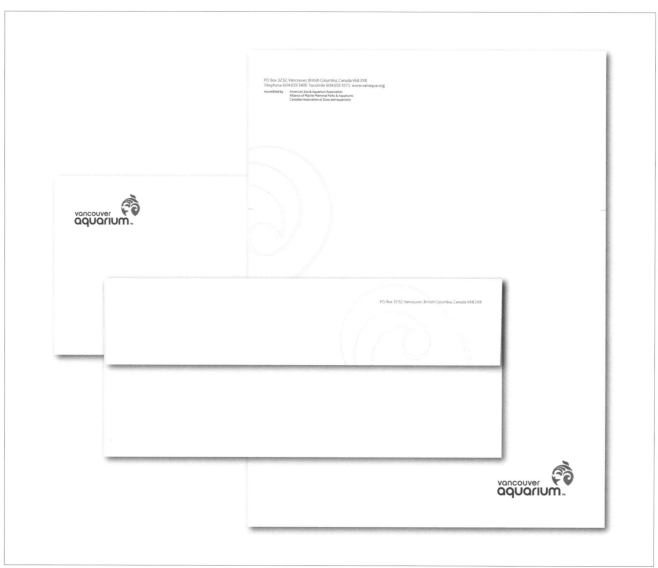

^ Redesigned envelope (front and back) and letterhead

distinctive and appropriate look that could be applied in almost every area of aquarium operations.

Inspired by the shape and spirit of earlier logos, the new icon Subplot Design created celebrates the aquarium's history and commitment to the conservation of aquatic life in its many forms. The main logo mark is that of a dynamic leaping fish and is made up of three smaller shapes representing aquatic fauna (sea star), flora (kelp) and the world of water (wave). The identity system grows out of sense of discovery, wonder and beauty of the aquatic environment. From new brochures to a refreshed website to new stationery, the aquarium's revitalized identity translates to all branded items and communications. Vivid photography of key flora and fauna provide beautiful backdrops to the brochures, main entrance signage, and additional collateral that highlights the Vancouver Aquarium experience.

^ Redesigned business card (front and back)

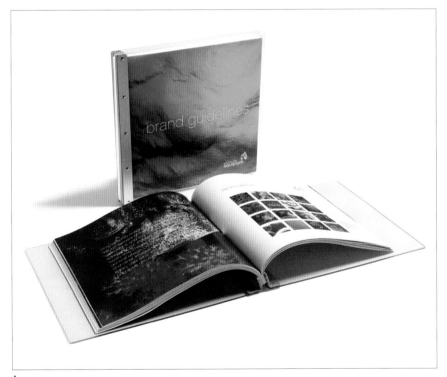

^ New graphic standards

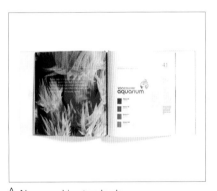

^ New graphic standards

ʌ Redesigned brochures

ʌ Redesigned wearables

ʌ Redesigned *Waters* magazine covers

ʌ Redesigned *Waters* magazine interiors

∧ New banners

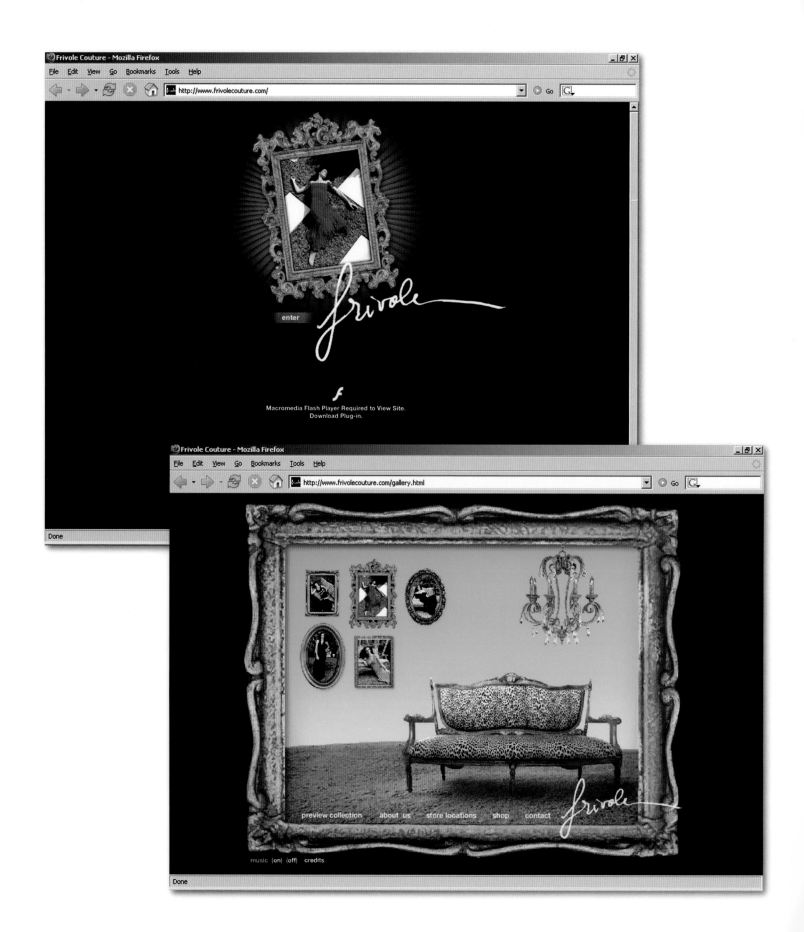

Frivole Couture

PROJECT:

FrivoleCouture.com
and Frivole.com identity
and website redesigns

DESIGN FIRM:

Breathewords

LOCATION:

Caldas da Rainha, Portugal

CREATIVE DIRECTOR/DESIGNER:

Adriana de Barros

"I'd like a functional, easy-to-use, incredibly sexy, elegant and interesting website," said client Neil de la Flor. With that, Breathewords began working on a thematic website for Frivole Couture's high-end fashion. The site, FrivoleCouture. com, featured a preview of the collection and a store locator. During its development, the designer created a logo for online use—a signature elegantly representing Frivole. The new treatment replaced a somewhat abstract *F* used as the previous identity. The company was so pleased with the new image that it decided to use it for all future branding.

The secondary redesign was building an e-commerce boutique for both men's and women's clothing (Frivole.com). The design firm customized all layout aspects, including the shopping cart checkout. The goal was to make a simple yet sophisticated fusion of commerce, fashion and entertainment. The boutique site made use of more traditional fashion photo imagery. The Frivole logo

⌄ Redesigned logo
<< Redesigned couture website pages

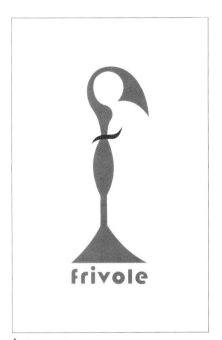

⌄ Previous logo

received a "diamond" graphic treatment for use on the boutique pages—to differentiate it from the couture website.

One of the most unique aspects of color usage on both websites is the use of black. Fashion directories and photo sites often use black, but it is uncommon for retail sites to use it. In Frivole's case, the black conveys a high fashion catwalk feel.

Ʌ Redesigned couture website page

Ʌ Redesigned couture website page

Ʌ Previous website page

Ʌ Previous website page

Ʌ Previous website page

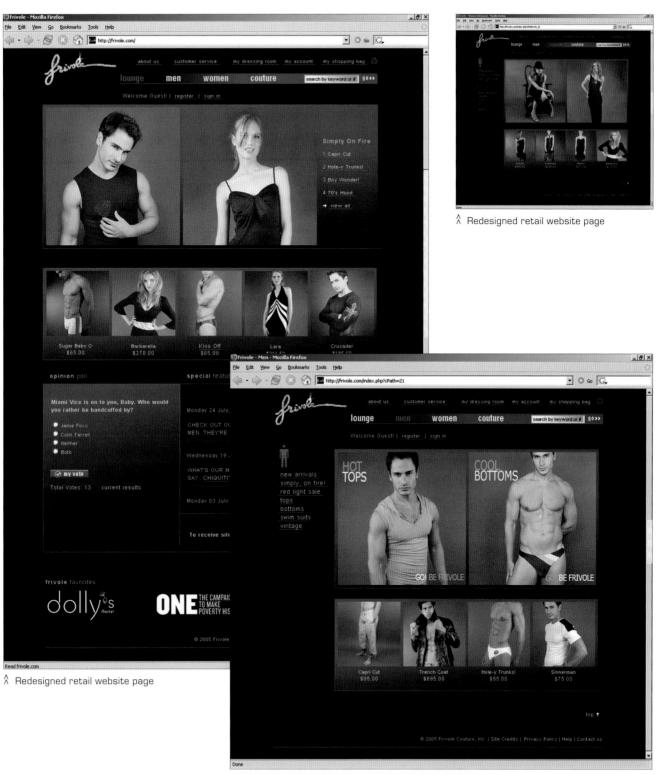

∧ Redesigned retail website page

∧ Redesigned retail website page

∧ Redesigned retail website page

THE BOYD CENTER
FOR INTEGRATIVE HEALTH
where healing begins

THE BOYD CENTER
FOR INTEGRATIVE HEALTH
where healing begins

D. BARRY BOYD, M.D., M.S., *Director* | T 203-869-2111

THE BOYD CENTER
FOR INTEGRATIVE HEALTH
where healing begins

The Boyd Center for | 15 Valley Drive
Integrative Health, LLC. | Greenwich, CT 06831

D. BARRY BOYD, M.D., M.S., *Director*

THE BOYD CENTER
FOR INTEGRATIVE HEALTH
where healing begins

Medical Oncology, Hematology, Nutrition & Internal Medicine

15 Valley Drive | www.boydcenter.com | T 203-869-2111
Greenwich, CT 06831 | dboyd@boydcenter.com | F 203-869-2203

The Boyd Center for Integrative Health, LLC. | 15 Valley Drive | Tel: 203-869-2111 | www.boydcenter.com
                                                        | Greenwich, CT 06831 | Fax: 203-869-2203 | info@boydcenter.com

The Boyd Center for Integrative Health

PROJECT:
Boyd Center logo and stationery package redesign

DESIGN FIRM:
b-design

LOCATION:
San Diego, California

CREATIVE DIRECTOR/DESIGNER:
Carey Jones

The directive for b-design was to make Dr. D. Barry Boyd's name the primary text in the business name and new identity. The new image was to convey a change in the practice to an integrative care program, including comprehensive wellness care, Western medicine and nutritional counseling. The new logo needed to reflect an empowered individual in the healing process.

The designer sketched numerous pages of different configurations. Variations stood alone and within various shapes. During the process, the circle became the most embracing and complete feeling for the outer shape. Within the circle element, the position of the arms swinging up to the right projected a sense of positive momentum. The hand-drawn treatment of the icon was used to symbolize individuality.

^ Logo concept sketches

^ Previous stationery

^ Redesigned logo
<<Redesigned stationery

^ Previous logo before name change

Murrays Jewelers - Mozilla

File   Edit   View   Go   Bookmarks   Tools   Window   Help

http://murraysjewelers.com/Index/bridal_showroom.php   Search

Murrays Jewelers

MURRAY'S
JEWELERS
handcrafted custom designed jewelery

Showroom
History
Services
Manufacturing
About Gems
Ask a Gemologist
Home

Bridal

14K White gold emerald cut solitaire engagement ring. Diamond
weighs .75ct. Style #1030 Price $3,995

FIVE GENERATIONS ~ SINCE 1885 ~ DOWNTOWN MUNCIE

113 W. CHARLES ST.
MUNCIE, IN 47305

Done

Murray's Jewelers

PROJECT:
Redesign of
www.murraysjewelry.com

DESIGN FIRM:
nHarmony, Inc.

LOCATION:
Muncie, Indiana

CREATIVE DIRECTOR:
Christina J. R. Hannah

Murray's Jewelers is a fine jewelry store with a rich heritage and creative flair for designing unique jewelry. Unlike many other jewelry stores, Murray's in-store selection is over eighty percent custom jewelry made on-site. Murray's has passed down the fine art of jewelry designing from generation to generation and has been located in Muncie, Indiana, since it first opened its doors in 1885.

Murray's Jewelers had a simple website with a few pictures of unique pieces, along with a company history and store location and hours. Murray's management felt that showing a larger selection of custom work online would draw more customers into the store and that a new design would help emphasize their image as an upscale, custom jewelry store.

nHarmony created a web design that reflected the richness of heritage and careful craftsmanship in Murray's Jewelry. The design is pleasing, yet does not draw attention from the true focus of the website—the jewelry itself. A virtual showroom makes it easy to categorize new jewelry and display with multiple views of each piece.

Videos of the jewelry-making process, made from an existing infomercial, were placed on the website so customers can see exactly how it's done. A special section on the front page allows Murray's to feature an item for prominent display. The content is easily changed as often as the client likes, and old features are placed into a special archive.

The new website has drawn many visitors who peruse the selection for an average of fifty-one page views per visit. Over 40 percent of the web visits are extended stays. Murray's reports that since the implementation of the new website, many customers have come into the store seeking a piece of jewelry they had viewed online first. Murray's Jewelers is extremely pleased with their new look and the showroom pages, and believe the website has increased traffic to their store.

^ Existing logo
<< Redesigned website page

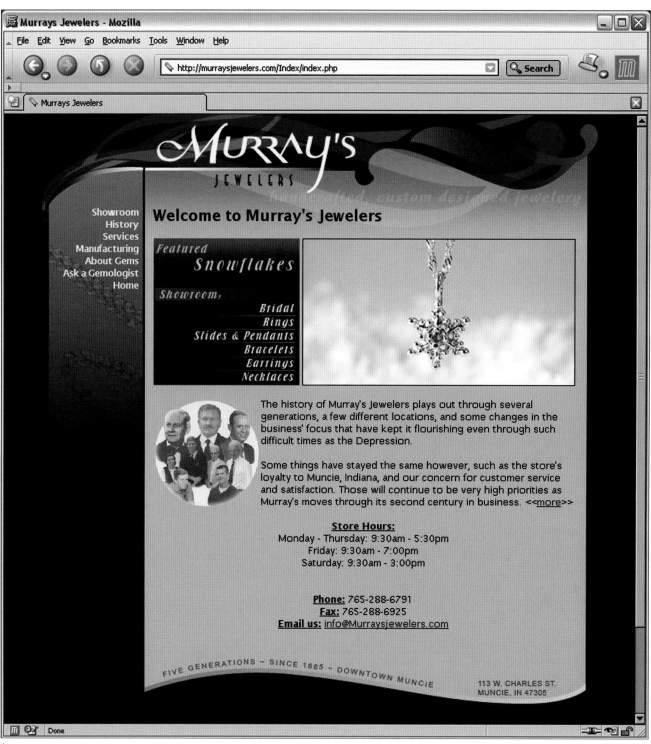

^ Redesigned website page

^ Previous website page

WORDS OF WISDOM

"Understand your reasons and needs for the change in the first place. Don't look at trend or at being fashionable as one of those reasons. Understand what you own, understand its value, and educate yourself as to the positive and potentially negative impact any change may cause. Make sure your designer is asking you the right questions about your business, your needs and your reasons for change before embarking on a new identity program."

Mark E. Sackett
Reflectur (formerly Sackett Design)
San Francisco/Los Angeles/New York City
www.reflectur.com

Weyerhaeuser Company

PROJECT:

iLevel identity program

DESIGN FIRM:

Hornall Anderson Design

LOCATION:

Seattle, Washington

CREATIVE DIRECTORS:

Jack Anderson, James Tee

DESIGNERS:

James Tee, Andrew Wicklund, Elmer dela Cruz, Holly Craven, Jay Hilburn, Hayden Schoen, Belinda Bowling, Yuri Shvets, Michael Connors, Larry Anderson, Chris Freed, Eric McFarlan

INTERACTIVE GAME:

Jamie Monberg, Chris Monberg, Nathan Young, Joe King, Jason Hickner, Adrien Lo, Amber Regan, Curt Collinsworth, Erica Goldsmith

Weyerhaeuser Company, a Fortune 200 international forest products company, engaged Hornall Anderson to analyze the current strength of various existing brands in the Residential Wood Products (RWP— a subsidiary of Weyerhaeuser) portfolio and to recommend a brand strategy for taking a new venture to market. The RWP reintroduction would be the largest brand launch in Weyerhaeuser's 106-year history.

Hornall Anderson recommended that RWP execute a formal internal brand launch in advance of its external introduction. The design firm prescribed a coordinated strategy and five-phase timeline. The first two phases were focused internally.

Phase 1: Disseminate the brand through top-down and peer-to-peer efforts by utilizing change agents from all levels and areas of the organization, seeding the brand to these audiences and leveraging them to influence others company-wide.

^ Redesigned identity
<< New introduction and launch brochures

^ Previous identity prior to name change

Phase 2: Implement an internal launch strategy by branding the culture (align values and norms, build unity and celebrate brand behavior); culturizing the brand (generate excitement and ownership, demonstrate brand personality and voice) and making the internal launch engaging and rewarding.

Phase 3: Strategically and productively launch the brand to the public at large by introducing iLevel (the new name for RWP) to its fifty largest home-builder customers and also at Weyerhaeuser's annual shareholders meeting.

Phases 4 & 5: Extend the external launch to highlight the functional benefits of iLevel—integrated building systems that lead up to fully integrated structural framing.

The creation of a new identity, merchandising, collateral materials, a brand launch movie, an internal game for associates and a website worked together to communicate iLevel's new vision.

The creative development for the iLevel program began with naming. The overall focus was to convey and elevate the new Weyerhaeuser brand, while depicting the company's forward thinking and the benefits of how it is creating better and stronger houses.

After choosing the iLevel name, the creative team incorporated the new identity with the idea of "block" design. The design had to be bold and easy to implement when applied to wood products in a simple stenciled manner. The final solution took shape as a solid rectangle.

^ New promotional collateral

^ New promotion displays

^ New French brochures

Letterforms play up the symmetry of the letters in the word *iLevel*. Also enlisted was the device of using the letter *i* as a discovered element, so it didn't resemble or mimic other brands like iPod and iMac.

Determining the color palette for the program began with a competitive audit conducted by the Hornall Anderson creative team. During this audit, the team identified which colors within the industry have a strong connotation. Since green is an original Weyerhaeuser color, the team

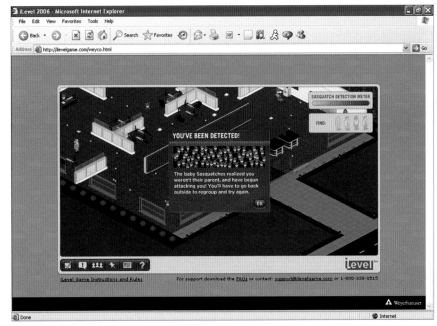

^ New online presence

decided to use the same color but to chose a different shade to tie back to the parent brand. As a result, the "iLevel green" is an ownable, easy, recognizable color—a brighter, more contemporary hue that not only complements the original Weyerhaeuser green, but also positions the brand toward a bolder future.

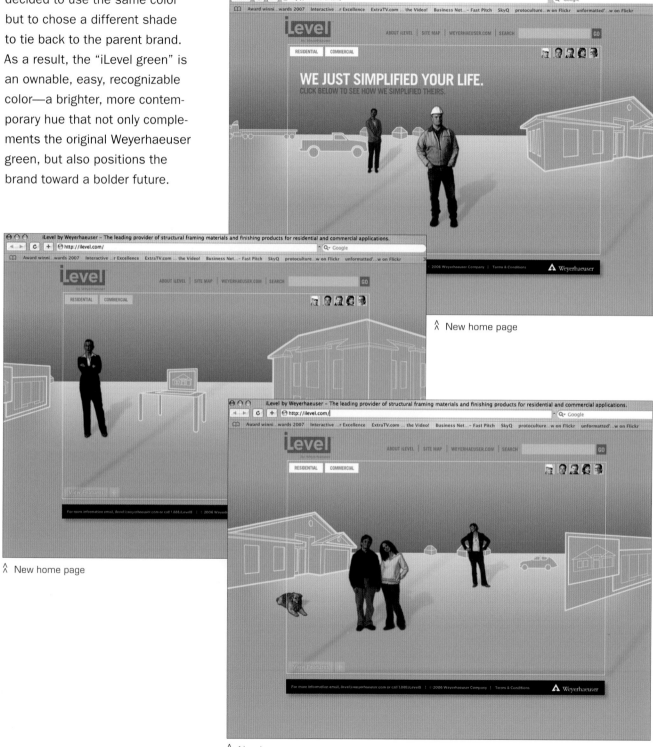

^ New home page

^ New home page

^ New home page

^ New web page samples

SLIPSTREAM
DESIGN

SLIPSTREAM
DESIGN

2101 9th Ave Suite 201
Seattle WA 98121
SlipstreamDesign.com

SLIPSTREAM
DESIGN

Drew Carlson
Principal, Industrial Designer
drewc@slipstreamdesign.com

2101 9th Ave Suite 201
Seattle WA 98121
tel > 206.783.4860
fax > 206.838.5295
SlipstreamDesign.com

2101 9th Ave Suite 201
Seattle WA 98121
tel > 206.783.4860
fax > 206.770.6130
SlipstreamDesign.com

Slipstream Design

PROJECT:
Slipstream redesign

DESIGN FIRM:
Modern Dog Design Co.

LOCATION:
Seattle, Washington

CREATIVE DIRECTOR:
Michael Strassburger

DESIGNERS:
Michael Strassburger,
Junichi Tsuneoka

Slipstream Design has developed products for companies such as Intel, Boeing, Microsoft's Xbox, VeriFone and Ride Snowboards. Ready for a more visible national presence, Slipstream called on Modern Dog to create a stronger image that better suited their vision and future needs. The new identity, colors and design components take cues from vintage tool packaging and are designed with enough flexibility to remain vibrant for years to come.

The project included logo, business papers and website design. In addition, Modern Dog is currently working on a promotional video, which they are producing, filming, editing and writing. The Slipstream video is used as a sales tool for potential clients and was completed in early 2007.

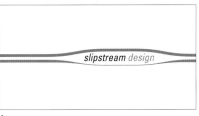

^ Previous logo

^ Redesigned logo

<< Redesigned envelope, letterhead, business card (front and back) and home page

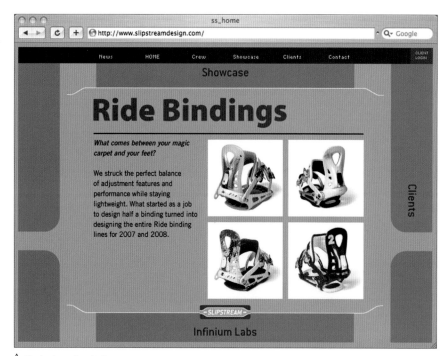

^ Redesigned website page

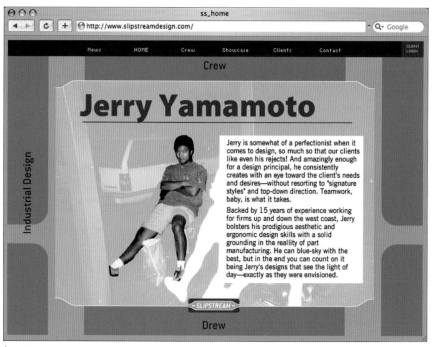

^ Redesigned website page

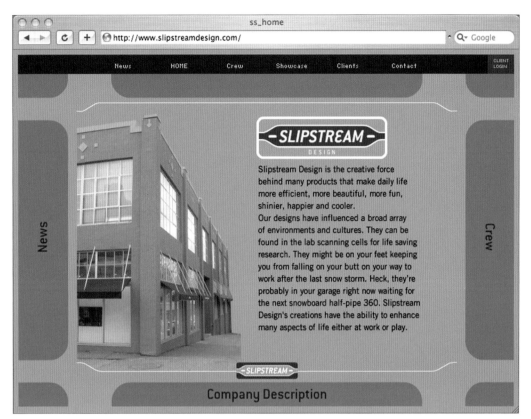

Slipstream Design is the creative force behind many products that make daily life more efficient, more beautiful, more fun, shinier, happier and cooler.

Our designs have influenced a broad array of environments and cultures. They can be found in the lab scanning cells for life saving research. They might be on your feet keeping you from falling on your butt on your way to work after the last snow storm. Heck, they're probably in your garage right now waiting for the next snowboard half-pipe 360. Slipstream Design's creations have the ability to enhance many aspects of life either at work or play.

Company Description

∧ Redesigned home page

WORDS OF WISDOM

"Take it slow, because if you're in a hurry, you'll overlook the bad idea that will later on become your favorite."

Robynne Raye
Modern Dog Design Co.
Seattle, Washington
www.moderndog.com

THE MAGAZINE OF
SIGMA CHI
WINTER 2006–07

Recognizing Milestones on
a common path

ANNUAL REPORT 2006

CLIENT IN CRISIS

Sigma Chi

PROJECT:
Sigma Chi identity

DESIGN FIRM:
Brainforest, Inc.

LOCATION:
Chicago, Illinois

ART DIRECTOR:
Nils Bunde

DESIGNERS:
Drew Larson, Jonathan Amen

In the competitive collegiate fraternity landscape, Sigma Chi and the Sigma Chi Foundation desired a more relevant, more inclusive presence. So one of America's oldest and most established fraternities brought in Brainforest to help with a complete brand makeover.

Starting with a redesign of the nineteenth-century crest, Brainforest developed a complete identity package to support a new Sigma Chi—and then applied that identity to a more user-friendly website, stationery and quarterly publication. The new dynamic image introduces both the fraternity and its foundation to the next generation of young men.

As is often the case when many divisions are in charge of developing materials, Sigma Chi did not have a single unifying visual identity system. Attempts had been made in the past to control the visual brand but had not been entirely successful. Brainforest understood that to get a large organization to change old habits, it needed to begin with buy-in. By creating a new identity that resonated with both the older Sigs and the newer prospects, the dedication to fraternal beliefs and the desired behavior would follow.

When dealing with a venerable institution, change must be slow and targeted. Beginning with mood boards, Brainforest worked with Sigma Chi to find their comfort level with change. In this way, they were able to move the fraternity to a more modern, progressive color palette, type choice, grid and crest.

And once they had the buy-in, applying the new look to a comprehensive system of materials was met with approval every step of the way. The result? A dynamic, user-friendly website, a clean and sleek system of stationery materials and a magazine that is as fresh and modern as the institution itself.

∧ Redesigned *Magazine of Sigma Chi* interior spread

<< Redesigned *Magazine of Sigma Chi* cover

ʌ Redesigned *Magazine of Sigma Chi* interior spread

ʌ Redesigned *Magazine of Sigma Chi* cover

ʌ Redesigned *Magazine of Sigma Chi* interior spread

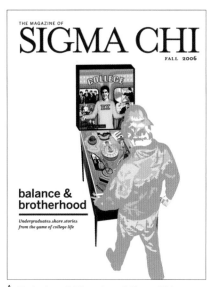

^ Redesigned *Magazine of Sigma Chi* cover

^ Redesigned *Magazine of Sigma Chi* interior spread

^ Previous *Magazine of Sigma Chi*

^ Redesigned stationery

^ Previous stationery package

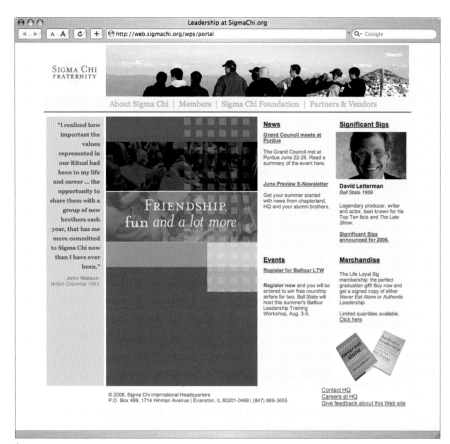

^ Redesigned website

^ Previous website

WORDS OF WISDOM

"Never tell a potential client (or existing client) that their logo sucks. There's often a good reason a firm, especially a smaller business, has used the same identity for a long period of time. In many cases, that logo image was created by a family member, long-time employee, or someone else closely connected to the firm. There's no need to alienate the client before a project even begins."

Jeff Fisher
Jeff Fisher LogoMotives
Portland, Oregon
www.jfisherlogomotives.com

AMERICAN TECHNION SOCIETY

TECHNION USA

SUMMER 2005

NOBEL
PRIZE
TO TWO
TECHNION
SCIENTISTS

AMERICAN TECHNION SOCIETY

TECHNION USA

SPRING 2007

TECHNION
GRAD STUDENTS
THE FACE OF
ISRAELI
HIGH-TECH
$1 BILLION
CAMPAIGN
LAUNCHED

American Technion Society

PROJECT:
American Technion Society
identity redesign

DESIGN FIRM:
Ellen Shapiro Associates, Inc.

LOCATION:
Irvington, NY

ART DIRECTOR/DESIGNER:
Ellen Shapiro

The American Technion Society provides financial support to The Technion, the leading science and technology university in Israel. Known as "Israel's MIT," the institution is educating future leaders in the life sciences, engineering, urban planning, water resource technology, computer science and medicine.

Shapiro Design Associates has been working with the ATS since 2002, designing its biannual magazine, newsletters and print collateral including folders, development brochures, ads and event invitations. This gave ATS communications a stronger, more consistent use of images, typography and color.

In the fall of 2006, the ATS board of directors expanded its $750 million campaign to $1 billion. The time was ripe for a logo redesign. The ATS logo had been essentially the same since 1940, when the organization adopted a variation of the Technion institu-

⌃ Redesigned logo
<< New *Technion USA* magazine covers

⌃ Previous logo and icon treatments

tional logo, the Hebrew letter *tet* with a flame.

Designer Ellen Shapiro experimented with a number of ideations of the letter *tet*, based on various Hebrew fonts. The *tet* is the initial letter of the word *tov, good*. The form of the *tet* is "inverted," thus symbolizing hidden, inverted good—suggesting the good is hidden, or can be found, within it. The challenge was to retain the shape and legibility of the letterform while making a handsome base or container for the flame, which was simplified to a single curve.

The name was also simplified: from "American Society for Technion—Israel Institute of Technology" to "American Technion Society." The typography, Trump Medieval, a classic roman face befitting a distinguished university, contrasts with the architectural simplicity of the mark.

Shapiro Design developed a stationery program and a set of nameplates for print and online publications. The new Identity Guidelines set forth correct uses of the logo in its various forms, and address color, typography and layout. The Guidelines, published in PDF format as well as printed digitally, can be used in-house, by other agencies and design studios, and by regional chapters when preparing their own materials.

"Our new logo is both modern and classic, like the Technion itself," says Martha Molnar, ATS director of communications.

"More important, it stands out boldly and distinguishes us from other organizations."

ʌ Various explorations in creating the redesigned logo

ʌ Redesigned letterhead and business card

⌃ New flag designs for various ATS publications

⌃ Redesigned brochures

⌃ New *Technion Wellness Report* newsletter format

Resources

BOOKS

More than mere volumes of just pretty identity and branding pictures, the following books are good resources for designers—and their clients—about the process of executing such projects.

Beyond Logos: New Definitions of Corporate Identity
Clare Dowdy
(Rotovision, 2003)

Brand Apart: Insights on the art of creating a distinctive brand voice
Joe Duffy
(One Club Publishing, 2005)

Branding: 10 Truths Behind Successful Brands
Robin Landa
(Amazon.com Shorts, 2006)

Branding: Brand Strategy, Design and Implementation of Corporate and Product Identity
Helen Vaid

(Watson-Guptill Publications, 2003)

Designing Brand Experiences: Creating Powerful Integrated Brand Solutions
Robin Landa
(Thomson Delmar Learning, 2005)`

Designing Brands: Market Success through Graphic Distinction
Emily Schrubbe-Potts
(Rockport Publishers, 2000)

Designing Brand Identity: A Complete Guide to Creating, Building, and Maintaining Strong Brands
Alina Wheeler
(Wiley, 2003)

Designing Corporate Identity
Pat Matson Knapp
(Rockport Publishers, 2001)

Global Graphics: Symbols— Designing With Symbols for International Markets
Anistatia R. Miller, Jared M. Brown & Cheryl Dangel Cullen
(Rockport Publishers, 2000)

How to Design Logos, Symbols & Icons: Internationally Renowned Studios Reveal How They Develop Trademarks for Print and New Media
Gregory Thomas
(HOW Design Books, 2003)

Identity Design That Works: Secrets for Successful Identity Design
Cheryl Dangel Cullen
(Rockport Publishers, 2003)

Identity Solutions: How to Create Effective Brands With Letterheads, Logos and Business Cards
Cheryl Dangel Cullen & Amy Schell
(HOW Design Books, 2003)

Logo Design That Works:
Secrets for Successful
Logo Design
Lisa Silver
(Rockport Publishers, 2001)

Logo Design Workbook:
A Hands-On Guide to
Creating Logos
Sean Adams & Noreen Morioka
with Terry Stone
(Rockport Publishers, 2006)

Logo Lab: Featuring 18 Case
Studies That Demonstrate
Identity Creation from Concept
to Completion
Christopher Simmons
(HOW Design Books, 2005)

Logo R.I.P.: A Commemoration
of Deceased Logo-Types
Declan Stone & Garech Stone
(BIS Publishers, 2003)

Logos: Making a Strong
Mark: 150 Strategies for
Logos That Last
Anistasia R. Miller & Jared M.
Brown
(Rockport Publishers, 2004)

Logos Redesigned: How 200
Companies Successfully
Changed Their Image
David E. Carter
(Harper Design, 2005)

Redesigning Identity
Catharine Fishel
(Rockport Publishers, 2002)

Stand Out from the Crowd:
Secrets to Crafting a Winning
Company Identity
Jay Lipe
(Kaplan Publishing, 2006)

The Secret Life of Logos:
Behind the Scenes With
Top Designers
Leslie Cabarga
(HOW Design Books, 2007)

What Logos Do: And How
They Do It
Anistasia R. Miller & Jared
M. Brown
(Rockport Publishers, 2000)

INTERNET LINKS

The Internet has become a valuable resource for the identity designer. The following are suggested online links for expanding one's logo design knowledge base.

A Web Site about Corporate Identity
http://users.ncrvnet.nl/mstol

The Best Brands of the World
www.brandsoftheworld.com

BrandChannel
www.brandchannel.com

Brand Infection
http://brandinfection.com

Brandmarker
www.monochrom.at/markenzeich-nen/index-eng.htm

Brand New
www.underconsideration.com/brandnew

Corporate Identity Documentation
www.cidoc.net

Corporate Identity Portal
www.ci-portal.de

Design Management Institute
www.dmi.org

GRAPHIC make-overs at
creativelatitude.com
www.creativelatitude.com/graph

The History of Branding
www.historyofbranding.com

Identityworks
www.identityworks.com

International Branding Association
www.internationalbranding.org

Logo Notions at creativelatitude.com
www.creativelatitude.com/logo_
notions

Logo R.I.P.
www.logorip.com

ReBrand
www.rebrand.com

Wireality
www.wireality.com

Directory of Contributors

3 Dogz Creative Inc.
Toronto, ON, Canada
www.3dogz.com
info@3dogz.com

Sean Adams
AdamsMorioka, Inc.
Beverly Hills, CA USA
www.adamsmorioka.com

Advertising By Design
Clermont, FL USA
www.abdfla.com

Jack Anderson
See Hornall Anderson
Design Works

angryporcupine*design
Park City, UT USA
www.angryporcupine.com
info@angryporcupine.com

Avenue Marketing
& Communications
Chicago, IL USA
www.avenue-inc.com
bdomenz@avenue-inc.com

b-design
San Diego, CA USA
www.b-design.net
carey@b-design.net

biz-R
Totnes, Devon, UK
www.biz-r.co.uk
look@biz-r.co.uk

Brainforest, Inc.
Chicago, IL USA
www.brainforest.com
creative@brainforest.com

Breathewords
Caldas da Rainha, Portugal
www.breathewords.com
info@breathewords.com

CC Graphic Design
Salt Lake City, UT USA
www.ccgraphicdesignstudio.com
Carolyn@ccgraphicdesignstudio.com

Common Sense Design
New Hamburg, ONT CA
www.commonsensedesign.net
Nigel@commonsensedesign.net

Connacher Design
Stamford, CT USA
www.connacher.com
nat@connacher.com

Bob Domenz
See Avenue Marketing
& Communications
bdomenz@avenue-inc.com

Finamore Design
Brooklyn, NY USA
www.finamoredesign.com
info@finamoredesign.com

FullblastInc.com
Portland, OR USA
www.fullblastinc.com
contact@fullblastinc.com

Glitschka Studios
Salem, OR USA
www.glitschka.com
info@glitschka.com

Graphicwise, Inc.
Irvine, CA USA
www.graphicwise.com
info@graphicwise.com

Hornall Anderson Design
Seattle, WA USA
www.hadw.com
info@hadw.com

Identityworks
Rye, NY USA
www.identityworks.com
spaeth@identityworks.com

Jeff Fisher LogoMotives
Portland, OR USA
www.jfisherlogomotives.com
logos@jfisherlogomotives.com

John Silver Design
Bothell, WA USA
www.johnsilveronline.com
john@johnsilveronline.com

Robin Landa
New York City, NY USA
www.robinlanda.com
robin@robinlanda.com

MasonBaronet
Dallas, TX USA
www.masonbaronet.com
holly@masonbaronet.com

Mayhem Studios
Los Angeles, CA USA
www.mayhemstudios.com
info@mayhemstudios.com

Debbie Millman
Sterling Brands
New York City, NY USA
www.sterlingbrands.com
www.debbiemillman.com

Modern Dog Design Co.
Seattle, WA USA
www.moderndog.com
info@moderndog.com

MyBrand, Consultores de
Negócios e Marketing, SA
Lisbon, Portugal and
London, England
www.mybrandconsultants.com
pedro.froes@mybrand.pt

nHarmony, Inc.
Muncie, IN USA
www.nharmony.com
design@nharmony.com

Octavo Designs
Frederick, MD USA
www.8vodesigns.com
info@8vodesigns.com

Paragon Marketing
Communications
Salmiya, Kuwait
www.paragonmc.com
info@paragonmc.com

Robynne Raye
See Modern Dog Design Co.
bubbles@moderndog.com

Rdqlus Design Quantum (RDQ)
Omaha, NE USA
www.rdqlus.com
info@rdqlus.com

Round2 Communications
Baltimore, MD USA
www.round2communications.com
davetaub@round2communica-
tions.com

Mark E. Sackett
Reflectur (formerly Sackett Design)
San Francisco/Los Angeles/New
York City, USA
www.reflectur.com
msackett@reflectur.com

Sayles Graphic Design
Des Moines, IA USA
www.saylesdesign.com

Shine Advertising Co.
Madison, WI USA
www.shinenorth.com
chanke@shinenorth.com

Sockeye Creative Inc.
Portland, OR USA
www.sockeyecreative.com
hello@sockeyecreative.com

Tony Spaeth
See *Identityworks*

Studio GT&P
Foligno (PG), Italy
www.tobanelli.it
info@tobanelli.it

Subplot Design Inc.
Vancouver, BC CA
www.subplot.com
info@subplot.com

Visual Language
Irvington, NY USA
www.visualanguage.net
info@visualanguage.net

Willoughby Design Group
Kansas City, MO USA
www.willoughbydesign.com
info@willoughbydesign.com

Jack Yan
Jack Yan & Associates
Wellington, New Zealand
www.jyanet.com
www.jackyan.com
jack.yan@jya.net

Index of Projects by Type

ACKNOWLEDGMENTS

It was necessary to go through a period of recovery after the completion of my last book, *The Savvy Designer's Guide to Success*. A little over two years after its release, I told my partner Ed that I felt I might be ready to take on another writing project. He mentioned that I should attempt to get another book lined up before we left for vacation a couple of weeks later. About the same time, my previous editor, Amy Schell, sent me an e-mail asking if I had any ideas for future books. She suggested I run any concepts I might have past HOW Design Books acquisitions editor Megan Patrick. One day I sent Megan an e-mail with some ideas, and by the middle of the next day, the book *Identity Crisis!* began to take form. I thank Megan for fine-tuning my initial thoughts, Amy for putting up with me again as my editor and the entire HOW staff for always being so supportive of my endeavors.

The inspiration for this book came from one of my partners-in-crime on the management team of CreativeLatitude.com. I need to send special thanks in the direction of our design diva, Alina Hagen. Her Graphic make-overs feature on the site gave me the inspiration for a "before and after"

book, and she graciously told me to run with the idea. While judging the Summit Creative Awards over several years I have been introduced to the work of several of the design firms included in this volume. I thank Jocelyn Luciano, executive director of the awards, for the opportunity to learn about the talents of these designers from around the world.

Thanks also to all the international graphic design professionals who were willing to share their design work, and knowledge. Your help was necessary to make this book a reality I also appreciate the willingness of their clients to allow their business' "Identity Crisis!" situations to be presented in such a public forum.

Parts of this book were written while traveling or visiting friends. I do need to thank those on whom I imposed, when I should have been enjoying their company, including my sister Sue and her husband A.J. in Benicia, CA; Karen, Jack and Susan while in Depoe Bay, OR; Mike, Lisa, Bev, Anne, Jon, Pierce and Erin at our gold-mining camp in Oregon's Wallowa Mountains; the ALA Oregon gang at the Cannon Beach, OR, house and at the Palm Springs conference;

Mike again for the use of his dining room table at his Joy Creek Nursery home; the gang at the Pavel "campground" in Molalla, OR; the Holland+Knight law firm business managers who wanted me to come out and play with them in Tampa, FL, as I finished the manuscript; and our great hosts Greg and Frank in Atlanta, who put up with me double-checking everything after it had been sent off and allowing me to begin my "author's rehab" program while at their home. Apologies to Shawn and Greg for missing so many of their Thursday night summer poolside "happy hours," due to nights of working on this book. Additional thanks to Bev and Lisa for allowing "work" to take place at the vacation house in St. Croix.

Special thanks to my Thursday morning Kaffeeklatsch gang of Myra, Ron, Don and Steve (and occasionally Michael) for trying to keep me a bit sane with a little weekly caffeine therapy. With three of the individuals in the group writing books, and one working on other writing efforts, we all needed just a bit of sanity in our lives.

And, of course, my gratitude to Ed.